Beautiful
Money

Beautiful Money

THE 4-WEEK TOTAL WEALTH MAKEOVER

LEANNE JACOBS

A TarcherPerigee Book

tarcherperigee

An imprint of Penguin Random House LLC
375 Hudson Street
New York, New York 10014

Most TarcherPerigee books are available at special quantity discounts for bulk
purchase for sales promotions, premiums, fund-raising, and educational needs. Special
books or book excerpts also can be created to fit specific needs. For details, write:
SpecialMarkets@penguinrandomhouse.com.

LIBRARY OF CONGRESS CATALOGING-IN-PUBLICATION DATA
Names: Jacobs, Leanne, author.
Title: Beautiful money : the 4-week total wealth makeover / Leanne Jacobs.
Description: New York : TarcherPerigee, [2017] | Includes index.
Identifiers: LCCN 2016036027 (print) | LCCN 2016047725 (ebook) | ISBN
9780143111511 (paperback) | ISBN 9781101992814 (ebook)
Subjects: LCSH: Self-actualization (Psychology) | Happiness. | Success. |
Finance, Personal. | BISAC: SELF-HELP / Personal Growth / Success. |
SELF-HELP / Personal Growth / Happiness. | BUSINESS & ECONOMICS / Personal
Finance / General.
Classification: LCC BF637.S4 J336 2017 (print) | LCC BF637.S4 (ebook) | DDC
158.1—dc23
LC record available at https://lccn.loc.gov/2016036027

Printed in the United States of America
1 3 5 7 9 10 8 6 4 2

Book design by Pauline Neuwirth

CONTENTS

The Path to Beautiful Money

WHEN MY CLIENT Aubrey started the Beautiful Money program, she admitted she was stuck. "I always pay my bills," she said when we first met, "but barely." As an entrepreneur, Aubrey turned a profit but wasn't getting ahead financially. If anything, she was on the verge of falling behind. She worried about her account balances, her business, and her future almost every day.

Like many of us, Aubrey had bought into the idea that working as hard as possible is the only way to achieve success. If your business needs to make more money, then you need to put in more hours. You need to *do more*. So that's what Aubrey did. She spent more and more time at the office. She ignored how tired she felt. She became obsessed with her schedule, trying to maximize every minute of every day. She spent less time with her family, friends, even her fiancé. But no matter how many hours she put in or how hard she worked, nothing seemed to help grow her business or make a difference in her bank accounts. Aubrey still got the same mediocre results. She knew that something had to give, but she wasn't sure what that something could be.

At some point in our lives, we've all felt like Aubrey. We know what it's like to check our bank balances with dread or to lie in bed worrying about debt when we know we should be asleep. We know the true cost of giving up time with our loved ones, our weekends, our vacation days, and perhaps even our sanity in exchange for a paycheck. We all know what it's like to hear people brag about being too busy, working long hours, or having to respond to e-mails in the evening. The message is clear: if we're not consumed by work, then we're probably not important enough at our job. If we're not drowning in e-mails, we're not going to get the promotion. And if we don't get the promotion, then we aren't doing all we can for ourselves or for our families.

It's easy to see how our culture prioritizes success. We are trained from an early age to strive to have it all—the spouse, the house, the car, the clothes, the career, and the kids. But even when we do accomplish our goals—at work, at home, throughout our lives in general—we don't find satisfaction in our achievements. We spend most of our time "busy being busy," but what we're actually doing is being busy just to be broke. Many people live a life of complete madness for a paycheck-to-paycheck existence. According to recent surveys cited by *CBS MoneyWatch*, approximately thirty-eight million families depend on their biweekly paycheck to survive. Even scarier is the fact that one in four of those families makes more than $100,000 annually.[1]

The truth is that no matter how many zeros our paycheck contains, most of us are not only financially broke but spiritually and emotionally broke as well. When our goals just keep getting bigger and farther away, without any end in sight, we end up constantly chasing success—until the day we find ourselves sitting in corner offices and big houses, feeling unhappy, broke, burned out, and unfulfilled.

I know. I've been there.

During my twenties, I did what I was supposed to. I chased the dream. I was married, working at a flashy *Fortune* 500 company, and earning a substantial salary. From the outside, my life seemed completely on track. I was married to a wonderful, successful, and kind man. He was my best friend. We lived in a nice house in a good neighborhood. I had a prominent position at a popular, well-known pharmaceutical brand and was studying for my MBA so I could further my own career. In my spare time, I was a competitive athlete who spent hours each day in the gym, training to run marathons.

To everyone in my life, I appeared accomplished and successful. I was well on my way to having it all. But inside, I was suffocating in an invisible prison. I had a good relationship with my husband, but we were outgrowing it. I felt like I was wearing golden handcuffs. I spent all my salary on stuff, because I felt like my life was completely void of passion and fulfillment. I was always busy, and I never seemed to have enough time to do anything I actually *liked* to do. Constantly pressured to put in longer and longer hours at the office, I didn't have the mental space to take care of myself, to make healthy meals, or even to spend time with my husband, much less nurture our marriage.

After years of living this way, one morning I woke up feeling completely empty, disconnected, and burned out. I couldn't even name one thing I was passionate about. I wasn't just exhausted on a physical level but on a spiritual one too. I felt deflated. I was bringing home a six-figure income but still living paycheck to paycheck. I was spending all my time at work, school, and the gym, so I didn't have a hobby or much of a social life. Every day I was rushing somewhere—to a meeting, to class, to the gym, to make a deadline. I felt like I was sprinting through my life. The tension in my body was constant; my fight-or-flight mechanism (I now understand) was always turned on because of the stress I made myself deal with on a daily basis. I barely slept. I lived off Diet Coke and protein bars. I would go to work at eight, stay until six, attend class four nights a week, go to a twenty-four-hour gym to get in an hour or two of cardio or marathon training, and then commute home sometime after midnight, only to drop into bed and do it all over again.

I call this time in my life my "starvation period" because I was literally starving, both physically and spiritually. I was eating nothing but empty calories, which didn't fuel my body. More important, I didn't feel like I was contributing to the world. I felt totally disconnected from my passions. I wasn't happy, and because of that, I was starving spiritually too. I had been living a lifestyle I was brought up to believe was important. I assumed I would be happy and fulfilled if I sounded successful on paper. But then I realized what I had been chasing wasn't me.

My dad calls this the "gopher syndrome"—essentially chasing your own tail and burning yourself out while trying to please other people or meet someone else's standard for your life. I didn't realize I was doing exactly that until one night, while lying in bed, I had a moment of clarity. Was the life I was leading all there was? What was the point of all this busy insanity? Why was I so willing to excel at things I disliked?

I hadn't had a truly connected and meaningful experience in years. I felt stuck, unhappy, and alone. My résumé may have been impressive, full of achievements and degrees and awards, but my soul felt empty. The next morning I seriously wondered if I had wasted the best days of my life trying to accomplish things that really didn't matter.

Still lying in bed, I had an epiphany. I didn't care anymore about getting to the next level on the corporate ladder. If my six-figure salary and impressive job title meant I would feel demoralized and unfulfilled for one more minute, it wasn't worth it. I wanted to feel free. I wanted my life to be rewarding and to help others. I wanted my body to feel light and strong at the same time. I wanted to prioritize myself, not spend my life making profits for someone else.

I began to think about how long I had been making choices that led me, over time, to feel unmotivated, empty, and rotten. Because I was consumed with chasing success and all its external accoutrements, I had allowed—chosen—to let other people dictate what I would do with my time, my money, and my thoughts. I was sitting in the passenger seat of my own life.

But I wanted—needed—to steer my life in a different direction. I wanted to feel more fulfilled, energetic, and happy. I didn't want a career in which someone else was in charge of my time or what I did on a daily basis. I needed time out, to recover from the burnout my corporate job had created. At the time, I didn't know what I would do exactly, but I knew that something *had* to change.

That was my first step on the path to creating Beautiful Money.

⌒

This book will be unlike any other financial guide you've read before. That's because the Beautiful Money mission is different. I aim to do more than just teach people how to budget properly and save for retirement (although I'll share advice on that too).

I have an audacious goal for Beautiful Money: to teach people around the world how to create holistic wealth. I aspire to teach as many people as possible how to stop chasing money and start creating joyful, healthy, and aligned wealth. I desire to teach people how to have a healthy, dynamic relationship with money and how that translates into holistic wealth, success, and alignment in every aspect of life. Having a positive relationship with money helps to increase our confidence, satisfaction, happiness, and what we're able to give back to our family, community, and the world.

What makes this book unique is that it will help you design a lifestyle based on what you value most, so you will no longer be chasing someone else's definition of success. Instead, you will be creating financial wealth while feeling inspired to create your greatest life—each and every day! Essentially, I teach what I had to learn the hard way: that when it comes to money, work, and success there are simple tweaks we can all make to our daily thoughts, behaviors, and habits that can lead to greater abundance, happiness, and satisfaction in our daily lives. True wealth is an inside job.

My Beautiful Money Moment

WHEN I DECIDED I couldn't live another day feeling burned out and stressed all the time, I went to my local bookstore. I browsed the self-help and personal finance sections, looking for a book that would show me how to manage the money I had while creating a lifestyle I loved. *But it didn't exist.*

I had already realized, somewhere deep down, that if I wanted to properly create and manage wealth, my lifestyle needed to reflect my core values. Looking back, even then I saw that true prosperity has to begin with a foundation of truth. I needed to ensure that my vehicles for making money were aligned with what brought me joy, inspiration, and passion. I needed to learn how to take better care of myself, and part of that was respecting myself, and my money, more.

Ten years ago, I simply knew that I felt out of sync with my work, my daily life, and my true self. That's when I decided to make a change.

By aligning our thoughts, behaviors, and feelings with what we truly desire, we give the universe and its powerful spiritual forces the opportunity to help us flow into our next level of leadership, peace, success, and joy with ease and incredible grace. At this point, you may wonder what the heck the universe and its spiritual power have to do with your finances. But don't worry; we'll get there.

What you need to know now is that if you follow the advice in this book, you can achieve absolute financial, emotional, and temporal freedom while experiencing a level of abundance you've never felt before.

My journey to Beautiful Money began the night I was lying awake staring at my bedroom ceiling, when I realized that I had spent far too much time chasing empty achievements. I had become chronically addicted to my to-do lists. With very little thought, I would just hustle and bustle to madly get all the day's to-dos checked off. I committed myself to no longer wasting time trying to achieve someone else's version of success. I quit my job the next day and never once looked back.

I set myself free, and my focus instantly shifted. There was suddenly *tons* of time to do what I had always wanted to do. I got rid of everything in my life that was no longer true for me. That, unfortunately, meant the end of my corporate career and the dissolution of my marriage. I was hungry for space, so I sold everything I owned. Once I had cleared my life of both emotional and physical clutter, I was able to breathe for the first time. That's when I decided to take a break from chasing after success and to really think about who I wanted to become as a person and what I wanted to do with my life. I was lucky enough to spend several months traveling through Europe on my own. When I returned home, I began to experiment with different activities and explore some of my passions, becoming an instructor in yoga and Pilates. I got certified as a clinical nutritionist and began a completely new career in direct selling, working for a wellness brand whose mission dovetailed with my own.

I overhauled my entire life, including how I earned and spent money. I gave years to building my own business and designing the way I live around what matters most to me: my freedom, my relationships, and my health. Today I'm financially free, married to the man of my dreams, and relishing my role as the mom of our four wonderful children. Our life is a great adventure, but we make sure to take care of our minds, hearts, and bodies. My husband and I strive always to include and prioritize what's most important to us.

In the Beautiful Money program, I will teach you how to lead from your heart and to be authentic to your innermost self, so you can live with grace in a place full of love—which is the opposite of how most people live (i.e., from a place of fear).

One of the best questions I ask my students is, "Are you living a life of greatness?" For most people, the answer is, "Not yet." A mentor of mine once said he could easily tell how a person thinks by asking her a few questions about her life: Think about how you are living. Are you happy? Do you wake up each day inspired? Do you set a clear intention for the day? Are you surrounded by amazing, abundant, and happy people? Are you living the life you truly desire? Or are you compromising and holding back in your life?

Most people settle for living small, for a variety of reasons. Most often we're afraid to fail, and we're also afraid not to be liked. We are afraid that if we really express ourselves and rock out our most abundant, authentic, brilliant, and aligned life, we will be unloved and alone. By letting fear lead and hold us back in our lives, we never really live. We never experience what it truly feels to be alive. What Beautiful Money will teach you is how to move yourself from the position you've been operating from—regardless of the fears that are in control—and slowly transition to a place of love, positivity, confidence, and inspiration. Beautiful Money comes with ease when your inner world is harmonious.

You might be thinking, "Leanne, this is *not* what I signed up for! I just want to learn how to get out of debt and make more money." And I totally get that. My path to developing the Beautiful Money program was long and winding, to be sure. I didn't know what I wanted in the beginning. I sold everything. I quit a job everyone else thought was awesome. I got divorced. I basically took the life I'd spent so much time and energy building, the life I'd hustled for, and threw it away. I was scared, but I was more scared to never experience the feeling of being alive and living on purpose.

My twenty seconds of courage birthed a more confident, powerful, clear, and happy woman. I ended up better as a result, financially, emotionally, and spiritually. This book is a shortcut to all the difficult lessons I had to learn the hard way. It is meant as a guide for you to follow on your own unique path to holistic abundance and financial wealth. By doing this work, you will learn how to reclaim your economic power and in the process create a greater and deeper connection with your true self. You'll see more cash in your wallet while also feeling more energized, motivated, happy, and fulfilled every day. Having complete financial and emotional freedom might seem like a faraway dream. But after seeing the Beautiful Money program in action with hundreds of clients, I know it's possible—if and when you commit to being in the driver's seat of your own life.

It's so easy to become complacent about our lives, our money, and our relationships. Life can get wildly busy! It's simpler and takes less time to just sit in the passenger seat and let the external environment drive us. Staying in the passenger seat allows us to avoid tough decisions, ruffling feathers, and possible failure. But it also keeps us from living a fulfilled, great, and juicy life. That's what was happening to Aubrey when she came to me, and what was happening to me during my starvation period, back in my twenties. Many people end up living unconsciously, driven by their habits or the expectations of people around them.

But we need to resist this urge to belong, to follow the pack just because it's simpler than forging our own way. Greatness lives outside the herd! We are each here to discover our own authentic and unique potential. We are each meant to lead in our own way, and if we don't get connected with that, if we don't question, be authentic, and give ourselves permission to go our own way (and maybe fail a few times doing so), we will never fulfill that destiny. We'll just be in the passenger seat of our life, letting someone else decide where we're headed. Imagine reaching the end of our time on this earth filled with regret because we lived our entire life according to what other people wanted. How would that feel?

The truth is that a lot of people live their lives hoping someone else will come along and give them the push to make a change—but that's on you! It's time to fully take ownership of your life and your results. Beautiful Money helps you do exactly that, by helping you move into the driver's seat of your life.

Consider Aubrey. After the Beautiful Money program inspired her to take the driver's role in her own life, she was able to change her behavior and watch her profits grow by 40 percent while cutting her time at work in half! Within weeks, Aubrey had not only stopped worrying about her finances but also achieved a savings goal that had eluded her for years.

Today Aubrey continues to achieve amazing returns, both professionally and personally. Her business has flourished, generating greater income and growing faster than ever before. She got engaged to the love of her life, and though she's on the verge of fifty, she feels like she's decades younger.

Most important, Aubrey has gained the confidence that her business will succeed. She walks away at the end of each day feeling secure about her own financial freedom. She takes days off without worry, without checking her in-box. She knows deep down that her approach to money has changed and that her new path is more holistic, helpful, motivational, practical, inspirational, and simply *beautiful*.

Anyone can use the techniques of Beautiful Money to create blissful, abundant, healthy personal and financial success. I've seen it happen—with Aubrey, with myself, and with the hundreds of other clients who have participated in my online courses.

In this book I provide the practical and spiritual guidance, tools, and strategies that can help you create and sustain the momentum necessary to make the biggest possible push for change in your life and financial situation. I've created this four-week program specifically to help anyone move into a higher state of wealth consciousness and design a lifestyle that is full of abundance, grace, generosity, and love.

By designing our days around what's truly important and valuable to us as individuals, we stand not only to increase the amount of money in our bank accounts but also to live in a heightened state of abundance, flow, grace, and authenticity every single day.

FOUR WEEKS TO FREEDOM: THE BEAUTIFUL MONEY COURSE

This course was created from my heart. It combines wisdom gathered from my own experiences with wisdom from my greatest mentors. The course outlines the exact steps I took to transform my life from Diet Coke and deficit to lightness, freedom, and alignment. What I've learned from developing and teaching the course over the past few years is that four weeks is the perfect amount of time to completely change your lifestyle. That might seem fast or overwhelming, but I've found that people tend to lose their momentum, energy, and inspiration if the program is longer. The truth is, when we need to change we (usually) want it to happen now.

So change starts today. The overall structure of the Beautiful Money course is strategic: we will work on cleansing your life of what isn't working before we design how we want your life to be. I've found that most people come to my program because their life is full of chaos, drama, and burnout. It's like holding a coffee cup that's completely full—if you add more, you'll just burn your hand. In the first few weeks, we look to decrease the amount your "cup" is holding, and then later we provide the tools that will help you move forward with a healthier cup of java, full of energy and motivation for positive change.

YOUR PATH TO BEAUTIFUL MONEY BEGINS NOW

Please know that there is no right or wrong way to practice Beautiful Money. As in yoga, the work itself is its own reward. If you consistently do the work, you'll reap both financial and emotional dividends. But how much effort you decide to put in—and how much reward you reap—is completely up to you.

The program is divided into four separate weeks. Each week contains three steps to implement during that time. Although Beautiful Money is designed so the whole program can be completed within a month, your pace may be different. If a step feels overwhelming, or if you'd like to take more time with a particular action, that's totally okay. We all have our strengths, weaknesses, and preferences. Some people fly through the first two weeks but find the third week harder. Others find the first two weeks difficult but the last two weeks easy to implement.

Whatever feels natural and safe is fine. I encourage you to check in with yourself but also not to shy away from stepping out of your comfort zone. Change may be uncomfortable, but it's the only way to unlock the golden handcuffs and restrictive habits we trap ourselves in.

Each week of Beautiful Money combines practical money management advice with exercises that help you figure out who you are, who you want to become, and how that correlates to creating better cash flow and more financial abundance. The program builds upon itself from week to week, helping to establish better, healthier habits and to reframe your relationship with money. Here is a general overview of what we'll cover from week to week:

In Week One we make gorgeous space. What do I mean by that? These initial steps will help you to figure out where you are and perhaps shed some light on how you got there. We'll set ourselves up for change and success by evaluating where we're starting from and by outlining principles that light our path forward.

In Week Two we create clarity about what we value in our lives and learn to focus our attention on only the things that we have set our sights on (instead of focusing on things we fear or don't want). During this second week, we begin to build our mental money muscles by shifting our thinking and feelings.

In Week Three we'll jump into action, rearranging and reorganizing our routine so our work prioritizes profits and positivity, and always reflects our core values. I'll share some exercises to minimize the fear that can arise when we have to take action, which will help build confidence and make it easier to implement both practical and emotional changes.

In Week Four we'll discover how we can all become money magnets. We will learn how to become more curious about our daily routines and identify ways to powerfully prioritize profits. An important part of Beautiful Money is discovering who you truly are and how to live authentically according to what's most valued and important in your life. This final week is about putting all the pieces together, aligning with your most authentic self and with harmonious prosperity. What are the few habits that create true wealth? What subtle internal shifts can open the doors to new levels of abundance? What areas in your life can be aligned with greater harmony and peace? How can each day be lived with intention? How can profit become a more powerful and peaceful priority?

READY FOR BEAUTIFUL MONEY?

If you know deep in your heart that you want and need *something more* or even *something less*—a different path, less chaos, more clarity, more peace, more fulfilling days, a better job, a more aligned lifestyle, a healthier bank account—then the Beautiful Money program is for you.

Remember, no matter where you're at, beauty, abundance, and grace are ready and waiting. Your job is to get clear about what you want and to make subtle tweaks to your lifestyle so you can live fully in your own power. The universal money taps are always turned on; we just need to dance in the flow. Every cell of your body is softly and graciously speaking to you at all times. Your natural state is one of well-being, abundance, grace, and love. Always listen to your body—whether it's a whisper or a scream, your body knows best. This is your time to dance, to write your own story, to find your own path to fulfillment.

Join the leading global community dedicated to holistic wealth, abundance, spiritual growth, authenticity, and alignment. Join Beautiful Money.

WEEK ONE

Make Gorgeous Space

THE BEAUTIFUL MONEY course has been created to teach people all around the world how to live in a heightened state of abundance, flow, grace, and authenticity *every day*.

In the first week of your transformation, we work on identifying where you are at today and what is holding you back from making change in your life. To create a life filled with joy, love, and abundance, you must make space for what you desire. But most of us lack the *space* and *clarity* required to make lasting changes.

This week, we'll work on clearing out the clutter. The act of making space and clarity creates an endpoint to work toward and the momentum to get there. Our mind can tell us that we want something—we can think, "I want to make more money," or "I want to have more free time to spend with loved ones," or "I want a job that aligns with my values"—but unless we are self-motivated to work toward that goal, we won't make it a priority.

One of my favorite TEDx talks is by author and motivational

speaker Mel Robbins. Mel explains why one-third of Americans feel dissatisfied with their lives. She says that the problem is a lack of clarity about what we really want. She believes our society suffers from "fine" syndrome. Instead of acting on a brilliant idea that would change our life for the better, we convince ourselves that we are fine. We choose to press our "inner snooze button" and do nothing. She says that our brain is neurologically wired to prefer what's easy, comfortable, and routine. Our work this week is to become crystal clear about what we truly desire.

We need momentum and space in order to have the energy to break out of our established routines and patterns. Clarity creates that momentum. It gives us a reason to get rid of what's no longer serving us, to go beyond what's comfortable, to live more consciously, and, overall, to be more aware of what's been holding us back from abundance. This first week of the Beautiful Money program involves three important steps that will help illustrate the concept of clarity and allow you to make the space necessary to break out of your established patterns.

First I'll explain the underlying principles of the program, which will redefine your approach to wealth and money management and help you to live more consciously.

Next you will evaluate where you are financially and emotionally, so you can have a clear picture of where you are at right now. I'll help you detach from wherever that is so you can move forward without obsessing about results, setting impossible-to-meet expectations, or beating yourself up about your current state. This second step is crucial, because it helps you detach from the emotional baggage that may be holding you back from making real, positive change.

Best of all, the third and final step in this first week is the Beautiful Money Cleanse. From deleting the e-mail in-box that makes you feel stressed to finally ditching clothes that you'll never wear, this holistic cleanse helps you figure out what *stuff* no longer serves you. By cleaning out your metaphorical and literal closets, you will increase the amount of emotional, mental, and physical space in your environment—and create the room necessary to make change.

By the end of these seven days, you will be living more consciously, actively creating clarity, and making space to move forward with new passion and commitment. Let's get started.

STEP ONE:
THE BEAUTIFUL MONEY PRINCIPLES

There are eight delicious principles to Beautiful Money. Like the program overall, each of these principles is created to help you transform knowledge into wisdom. This only happens when we take action and apply what we learn. Each principle helps to demonstrate how you can strengthen your mind-set and how simple actions can transform your mental money muscles. Each of these core principles will shape how you approach your finances and a new, conscious, self-aware way of living. By learning and incorporating these principles into your daily life, you can create Beautiful Money in an aligned, authentic, and mindful way.

The eight Beautiful Money principles are rooted in an essential truth: that our individual relationship with money is always an external projection or manifestation of our internal relationship with ourselves. How we treat, respect, discuss, use, or abuse money is a real-life measure of our own self-worth.

As such, money can be your greatest teacher when it comes to redefining, improving, and deepening your relationship with yourself, as well as understanding what drives your behavior. By incorporating the Beautiful Money principles into our daily lives, we truly begin to see what's working for us, as well as how we're working against ourselves.

By illuminating the beliefs and patterns that are no longer serving us, while simultaneously improving our relationship to money (and our most authentic selves), the eight Beautiful Money principles create a powerful clarity that resonates far beyond this program. These principles are the foundation of how to reshape your relationship with money so you can live more consciously and create abundant wealth without burning out or chasing someone else's definition of success.

This first step will help you begin this program with the clarity, focus, and knowledge necessary to set the stage for your next level of spiritual and financial success. If you practice and consciously incorporate these principles every day, you'll begin to live more consciously and authentically, which attracts even more momentum and helps to create wealth.

PRINCIPLE ONE: MONEY CAN HEAR YOU

This concept might seem fluffy for a financial guide, but I believe that the universe (or God) is always paying attention to the details of our day. I like to teach clients that someone is always watching (even when you think you are alone). The words you speak (and think) when it comes to money—saving, spending, investing—become the house and the environment you live (or die) in. Think about it: What do you say about money? About spending? About saving? About your wealth or lack thereof? Think about how your body feels (and how you feel) when you talk about money. Words have their own energy states. When we use low-frequency money words (such as "can't," "broke," "never," or "hard"), we don't feel good. If we listen to our bodies, these words just don't feel right coming out of our mouths. When they become habitual—"I'm always broke"—we ignore or numb our feelings. Over time, when we use phrases like "I can't afford it" or "It's so hard to make money" or "I will never be wealthy" often enough, we prime our brains to believe they're true.

Once these words become our normal and repetitive language, we subconsciously identify with their meanings. We become "broke" as people. They become part of how we define ourselves as human beings. It becomes completely normal for us to throw out these negative words without consciously feeling the low vibration they create. When we are fully present and aware, living consciously, speaking these words just doesn't feel good.

What's even worse is that when we attach ourselves to these words and the energies related to them for years, or even a lifetime, they become our reality. And that's the belief system we pass along as our legacy. For parents, these words become beliefs that are passed along to their children.

The first principle of Beautiful Money, "money can hear you," is about being loving and brave enough to be truly honest with yourself about what you say. It's about creating self-awareness to recognize that the words you use in relation to money have power.

OBSERVE YOURSELF:

How do you talk to others about finances and wealth?

What do you say to yourself? What do you say to other people?

What are the specific words that you use?

HOW POSITIVE OR NEGATIVE IS YOUR "MONEY TALK"?

Rate yourself from 1 (never) to 5 (often):

____ Money stresses me out

____ I am afraid I won't have enough

____ I will always be in debt

____ I am afraid of money

____ I fear managing money

_____ I am afraid to have too much

_____ I avoid my money situation

_____ I am not worthy of wealth

_____ You have to be great at sales to make lots of money

_____ You have to compromise your values to create wealth

_____ You have to become a workaholic to create wealth

_____ I am leery or jealous of wealthy people

_____ Wealth will change me

_____ Money is confusing and complicated

_____ I will lose friends if I create wealth

_____ I am too busy to create wealth

_____ I don't know enough to create wealth

_____ I don't have the right people around me

_____ I am destined to stay at the status quo

_____ I am angry at money

_____ I don't have what it takes to create wealth

_____ I am afraid of losing money

_____ I spend as a way of avoiding emotions

_____ I fear having to financially take care of myself

_____ I am dependent on others for money

_____ I lose sleep over money

Add up your scores, and check out what your money talk says:

Score: 26–55

You speak the Beautiful Money language! You are living with lightness and abundance when it comes to money. You are right on track and are doing phenomenally. With some fine-tuning, financial greatness is within your reach. Work on creating more clarity and space, as well as stepping even further out of your comfort zone when it comes to your finances and income streams. Make creating clarity in your life a daily intention. This program will help you challenge yourself to soar even higher, to create even more light and freedom.

Score: 56–90

You seek Beautiful Money but some mental, emotional, and physical clutter may be holding you back from a more joyful, more abundant, more connected relationship with money—and we'll address this later in the program. The brilliant news is that you are exactly where you are supposed to be: primed for greatness. You are ready right now for an entirely new level of abundance and success. Replacing old habits with new ones, using money mantras, and creating greater clarity and focus will be key. Pay attention to the principles and the lessons over the next two weeks because you're about to flow more and force less!

Score: 91–130

There is no better time than today to commit to a new chapter in your relationship to money. Remember that you deserve the best and are destined for greatness. It's time to stop avoiding your emotional relationship with money. Release your issues from your tissues. Take a deep exhalation and get psyched for the abundance that is on its way. Forgive yourself for any bad money habits or management in the past and commit to a successful, bright, empowered new beginning starting *right now*. Regardless of your circumstances, you are in the driver's seat and in charge of your results starting today. Take the leap from riding in the passenger's seat and start plotting your own path! Your work will be to let go of any past mistakes and judgments and clear your mental and emotional slate for a fresh and fun beginning. Be gentle and kind with yourself. You are right on track and on schedule.

The way we talk about money is driven by subconscious beliefs that stem from the ways the people around us—our parents, family, social circle, peers, even coworkers, acquaintances, and the media—talk about finances and wealth. The money conversation that took place around us while we were growing up also has a tremendous impact. Our experiences as kids etched deep money beliefs into our subconscious. These beliefs create our current reality around money. Most of the time, we aren't even aware of why we do what we do with our money. Our subconscious beliefs and habits have a fascinating ability to run our lives without us even being aware. They allow us to live our entire lives on autopilot, and if we don't create a deep sense of self-awareness, time flies by with us feeling victimized. Our work is to bring these "hidden" beliefs to the surface. After taking the quiz, my client Beth realized her money talk was casual to a fault. She had a tendency to buy lunch for her friends, to pay for rounds of drinks, to book all the hotel rooms for trips with her family—and never ask to be repaid. She told me that she always used to say things like "It's no big deal," or "You can't take it with you," or "It's just money." But when Beth actually analyzed her money talk, she realized that she was sending the universe a clear message that she didn't value money. Worse yet, she was also communicating that she didn't value herself enough to ask her friends and family to pay their fair share. "I was buying companionship," she admitted. And Beth is not alone.

In order to change how we talk about money, we need to acknowledge that we have been sitting in the passenger seat in our own lives. Our habits and beliefs have been in the driver's seat, instead of our true, authentic, and powerful selves. Once Beth became aware of how she was talking about money, she simply stopped offering to cover the tab for everyone else. "It was hard at first," she told me. "But my friends and family were happy to pick up the tab. One friend even said she was happy to pay for once!"

Observe how you talk about money for a few days. Try not to judge yourself; just observe the thoughts and communications that occur over the course of a few days. If there are obvious areas where you could improve—as there were for Beth—try to change an area at a time. It may be difficult, but learning to talk respectfully and positively about your money is an important step in creating wealth and abundance.

PRINCIPLE TWO: ASK FOR MONEY

A few months ago, my husband, Ric, and I ended up in a cashflow bind. We had started home renovations but ran into unexpected expenses far beyond what we had budgeted for. We'd planned well for this renovation: we had a good budget and a healthy surplus fund (in case we exceeded that budget) and trusted we were in good hands. But as much as you plan and prepare, sometimes the universe delivers the unexpected. We ended up needing an additional forty thousand dollars in our bank account within a few short weeks, and had no idea where that money would come from. I knew I had the skills to get to work and get busy making money. But I also knew that I was sleep deprived (having had three babies in less than three years) and emotionally exhausted. I just didn't have the energy to hustle to make extra income in an authentic way. If I did go ahead and burn the midnight oil the way I used to, it would not be in alignment with well-being and mindfulness. My health, family, and soul would suffer. For once, my solution wasn't to get busier and jump into action; it was to let go and allow. I decided to ask for money on a more global scale. I said, "Okay, universe, we need forty thousand dollars."

Bit by bit the money trickled in, from places we wouldn't have expected. I received a check for work I had done years ago and had completely forgotten about. Our passive income streams grew, and out of nowhere Ric received a few extra, well-paid corporate gigs. Gradually we built up the money we needed. We were confident, we trusted, and we asked for money—it was as simple as that.

Now, I'm not saying that the universe is an eternal piggy bank or that you can create wealth by simply asking and hoping for it. We can't live from a place of passiveness and weakness and expect money to roll in. But we can ask the universe for money when we need it and be clear about exactly how much money we desire. We can do our part and also ask the universe to assist us along our path. Having a vision and a plan is fundamental to creating wealth, but letting go is an equally important part of the process. We are often afraid to fully surrender, to "let go and let God." We forget that there is a higher power who wants us to thrive. We must remember to trust and have faith that we are meant to succeed in life. If we trust our gut and our heart, we simply cannot fail. Similarly, when an opportunity arises to ask someone else for money, we need to ask for what we're truly worth. The universe has our back, but it requires us to be clear and to ask.

Think about it. Have you ever really asked yourself, What are my skills, intelligence, and capabilities *truly* worth? I work with many gifted entrepreneurial clients who struggle with asking others to pay the amount of money their time is truly worth. Whether negotiating a salary or submitting an hourly rate, most of us have trouble asking for money. That's because there is an intensely strong correlation between dollar bills and how we value ourselves as individuals. We're taught by society not to be too self-confident or to "brag" about our abilities, so when it's time to negotiate pay, we lowball our amazing and powerful selves as a way of being polite or humble.

My client Beth just ran into this problem—with her husband! She had been offered a contracting gig at the retail company he works for. When her husband, Andy, asked what rate she would charge, Beth replied, "One hundred fifty dollars per hour, as usual." Andy told her that he thought the hiring managers would balk, and suggested that she lower her rate to one hundred per hour. But Beth followed the Beautiful Money principles, stood her ground, and asked for her usual rate. Though her new manager did come back and negotiate a slightly less lucrative deal, Beth still charges more than what her husband advised her to settle for. She asked for what she was worth and negotiated reasonably from there, even though it was uncomfortable.

I've heard similar stories from clients across the globe, in myriad industries, both entrepreneurial and corporate. This principle helped Beth "feel more confident and comfortable to ask for money in my work and business." She says, "I decided that it's time to earn my worth."

Following the principles of Beautiful Money will help you learn to be more comfortable with discomfort. We can't continue to do what we have been doing if we desire greater abundance, joy, and fulfillment in our lives. For me, when I started out as an entrepreneur, I found it really uncomfortable to negotiate my own deals and ask for money. I had to learn how to stand up for myself and be committed to asking for my full worth, despite how uncomfortable it made me feel. After feeling the discomfort a few times, I began to realize that people *would* pay what I was worth for the services I offered. Eventually, I came to realize that most of my clients still felt like they were getting an amazing value even at full price!

Offering your skills, abilities, and time at a discount doesn't serve anyone. You are basically pimping yourself out and proclaiming to the universe that you are always on sale and discounted! Your clients won't realize that they're getting a "deal," and subconsciously you're sending a message to yourself that you're not worth the money you truly deserve and the rate you've worked hard to achieve. You put the time in, gaining experience and credentials, so you should charge accordingly. If a client or an employer balks, that's their loss.

Changing how you ask for money—and becoming more comfortable with charging the full amount of what you are worth—will not only boost your income but also build your confidence that you deserve every penny. Trust me: this principle will lead you to more lucrative deals, less time at work, and higher confidence in yourself. The true message of this second principle is to stop messing around with your money. There's no need to make this journey harder than it needs to be. Learn how to ask for money, and get used to asking for it out loud!

PRINCIPLE THREE: RESPECT MONEY

Up until now, you may not have been the most responsible person when it comes to money—and that's okay. But moving forward, we need to remember that how we manage the pennies and dollars that come our way sends a message to the universe about whether we're ready to handle more. How we handle our money right now, in this moment, determines what financial rewards will come in the future. If we want to be rewarded with abundance, we need to show the universe that we can handle and respect the money we already have. If our wallet is messy and the bills are crumpled up, it is time to clean up and stop neglecting both our wallets and our lives. Maybe it's time for a beautiful new wallet that makes you feel divine, abundant, and wealthy. It doesn't have to be a Dior wallet (but if it fits your budget, do Dior!).

Practicing this principle completely changed the way my former client Kylie handled her money. She had decided to spring for the Beautiful Money course even though she could barely afford it, because she had always struggled with managing money. After declaring bankruptcy when she was twenty-eight, Kylie had completely given up using credit cards, but she was still spending every penny she earned.

After we discussed the Beautiful Money principles, Kylie decided on her own to enforce a ten-dollar weekly limit on what she called "fun money." Anything that was not related to necessities fell into that category. Dinner with girlfriends was a necessity, for both social and nutritional reasons, but a glass of wine at that dinner? Fun money. Taking a taxi when she could have taken a bus? Fun money. Buying a latte at a coffee shop when she could make a pot of regular coffee at home? Fun money. Taking an extra twenty dollars out of the ATM? Fun money.

Within two weeks of following what she called her "fun money allowance," Kylie saw the difference in her bank account. Though she loosened up her restrictions after a month—she allotted fifty dollars a week for fun money instead of just ten—Kylie realized how powerful respecting money could be. By being more mindful of what she spent her money on, Kylie was able to curb unnecessary spending and show the universe that she was ready for abundance.

By respecting money, we show the forces at play that we are capable of receiving more. After practicing her fun-money budget for two months, Kylie secured two major jobs for her business, which had never happened before. She was superexcited to tell her classmates in our seminar about her success. Learning how to respect her money taught Kylie an important lesson: money has an incredible power to impact our daily lives. It can be a force for good, but not if we waste what we've been given.

So ask yourself: have you respected money in the past? If not, what actions could you take to show the universe that you're ready to change how you handle what you are given? Remember that the universe is always watching you (in a loving way, of course). Where have you been neglectful, both when it comes to money and in other areas of your life? This third principle is about noticing neglect, giving those areas attention, and cleaning them up. Allowing mindlessness to creep into your life always, always, always shows up in your money management habits—and not in a good way. Energetically kiss those dollars and cents as they make their way into your stunningly organized wallet!

PRINCIPLE FOUR: CREATE WEALTH; DON'T CHASE MONEY

Western culture encourages us to get more money by any means necessary. Whether it's putting in a sixty-plus-hour week at the office or pursuing a career we don't love just because it pays well, most of us have been in a state where we're constantly chasing after money. But when we do that, we are usually living a lie. Why? Because it doesn't feel right, yet we do it anyway. This is the philosophy that everyone else is doing it, so we may as well do the same and fit in. We quiet our hearts and raise the volume on our busy, chaotic, and messy lives. It's time to step up, step out of fear, and live heroically. It's time to live a happy and fulfilled life. Think of every time in your life when your body has told you to slow down, rest, and listen to the music, but you chose to ignore that inner voice and pound life's pavement instead.

So many people get caught up in doing crap in pursuit of success. I love what business expert and entrepreneur extraordinaire Gary Vaynerchuk says about success: that in this day and age there is "no reason people should do shit they hate." But so many people do! A friend of mine recently attended her high school reunion and caught up with a friend named Courtney. Courtney was working in health care, which she hated, and studying for a better job as a physician's assistant, which she already knew she wouldn't like, and meanwhile racking up student-loan debt like there was no tomorrow—all because her family had convinced her that the field she's passionate about doesn't pay well. It was completely obvious to my friend that Courtney was desperately unhappy, but it was also clear that no one could convince her to stop following her family's so-called advice. Unfortunately, this is all too common: many, many people live their entire lives according to what other people want for them.

I recently visited New York City, which is a microcosm of this principle in action. What makes the Big Apple so different from anywhere else in the world is its energy. You can feel it the minute you get off a plane or train, or step onto the street in the morning. That energy can be positive: hustle and ambition and creativity. But after a few days there, I always start to notice a negative undercurrent of chasing and forcing and stress. As my friend Scott says, in Manhattan you can go from living to simply surviving pretty quickly. And surviving is no way to live.

Whether it's intentional or not, chasing money or success means that we're living passively and from the passenger seat in our own lives. When we do what we're "supposed" to do, when we choose to follow a path other people dictate is "right," we ignore our own desires and instead get completely caught up in achieving unimportant goals. Visionary leaders make decisions quickly but are slow to change gears or revise their plans based on the opinions of other people. They make their decisions based on intuition, on a sixth sense, and trust in their judgment. They have faith. They understand that opinions are a dime a dozen and create noise and chaos in one's path. Don't get me wrong, seeking wise advice from others can be helpful, but be very careful that those you seek advice and opinions from are true experts in the area you're asking about. When I hired a personal trainer in my early thirties, I sought out the best. I wanted to be trained by the fitness expert who was at the very top of her field. I have made this a practice. If I am seeking advice or guidance, I look to the best for advice. This not only helps me stay on course but also challenges me to live out of my comfort zone. Opinions from friends and family can be nice but are often rooted in fear. Not always, but often, friends and family are afraid that if you dare to soar in your life, they might lose you. This is why you will often get "Debbie downer" type of feedback when you go to them with a great idea, a new venture, or an intuitive calling. Essentially, we spend all our time doing shit we have no interest in doing because we all feel pressure to increase our salary year after year, to have a better-paying job, to meet someone else's expectations—to achieve, achieve, achieve at all costs. But what we need to realize is that living this way is unsustainable not only because of the physical and emotional stress it creates but also because of the spiritual heaviness it brings to our daily lives. We must remember that most people have good intentions but are busy dealing with their own shit. Even our closest friends don't have the time or mental space to have big visions and intentions for others.

The dynamic between chasing money and creating wealth is almost like the two sides of a coin or a swinging pendulum—you're either on one side or the other. When we surrender to the fact that money and wealth will come if we allow the universe to take over, we remove the negative emotional weight that constantly being in the rat race creates. By stepping out of the chase for success and money, we open up space for spiritual forces to come in and begin creating wealth.

My client and friend Linda realized that she was constantly chasing money. She told me that this principle of creating wealth rather than making money changed her perspective. "Most of society hears 'work hard' and 'grind it out,' so we end up in this chase. The idea of 'creating wealth' was exciting to me because I literally felt relief . . . I didn't have to go and go and go anymore. I was able to really look at my vision, look at my family's monthly income goals, and create the time freedom we wanted. When I'm following this principle, I feel lighter, more calm, and completely confident that we'll achieve our monthly goals every single time."

Admittedly, creating wealth instead of chasing money can be difficult to put into action right away. And it may seem awfully woo-woo to some of you. But my point is that we shouldn't be striving for someone else's definition of success in any aspect of our lives. We shouldn't chase down money or settle for surviving, either. We should stop doing the crap that doesn't matter, the work we hate, and pursuing goals that have no purpose or benefit. (In the next chapter, I'll explain more about how to do this!)

Instead, try to focus on the work that calls to us, that we're passionate about, that creates a positive effect, however small, on our world and those around us. We should pursue our vision for our own lives, no matter how crazy or how negative others are about it. The most difficult but most powerful first step is to commit yourself to living authentically and not according to the opinions of other people. By stepping out of the gutter full of crap that often fills our lives, we create room for greatness to step in. Believe in the process. We're going to learn how to get connected, get creative, and live totally authentically. We will learn to pursue wealth in alignment with our core values and our true selves. Our hearts will always guide us to Beautiful Money should we be bold enough to fully listen. We will discover that true wealth is an inside job.

PRINCIPLE FIVE: BE CLEAR ABOUT YOUR INTENTIONS

Clarity is the master key to Beautiful Money. We all know people who always seem to be busy, who always have a million things to do, who always seem stressed no matter what the situation. But when you look closer, what are those people so busy doing? Is your friend who stays late at the office doing important work that moves her toward her dream job or is she just managing chaos? The great failure is that we are addicted to, and obsessed with, being busy. Society as a whole is busy being broke. And those who have lots of money, what is their excuse for being so busy? I believe it is an addiction to busyness. As Tony Robbins mentions, achievement without fulfillment is failure. This was my aha moment. This was truly my Beautiful Money moment—my wake-up call.

What that obsessively busy person is missing (usually) is clarity. Without clarity, we end up constantly chasing something other than our dreams (usually our own tails!). And we never know what that "something" is. We are just stuck on repeat, like a mouse on a wheel.

However, when we have clarity, we become laser focused on achieving what we want and forgetting the rest. We all know someone who isn't frazzled, who always seems relaxed, who can always make time. You may describe them as "lucky" or "effortless." It might seem like all these awesome things just happen in their lives. But what's really going on with so-called lucky people is that their intentions are clear. These individuals are good at saying no to the good in order to say yes to the great, because their goals and priorities are clear. The intention behind their goals is positive and not ego driven.

For example, I wanted to write this book to help others create holistic wealth. My intention behind writing the book was not driven by ego (seeking fame, fortune, or praise). Money is wonderful and will absolutely be welcomed with an open heart, but it was not the key driver in writing this book. I believe when you create from the heart, money will follow (as long as you learn and apply the principles!).

To create Beautiful Money, our goals should be positive, serve others, contribute to the world, and be driven from a place of love, not fear. Developing clarity from a positive, helpful place allows us to create boundaries that are absolutely essential for the alignment that makes Beautiful Money.

When we are crystal clear, we attract less drama because we simply don't have time for it. Drama needs attention to thrive. Creating clarity in our lives takes our attention from anything that's not directly on the path to our goal. So when we have clarity,

drama dies on the vine. And even when some drama does occur—
because that's life—we have the emotional capacity to handle it.

So how do you know when you have clarity in your life? You feel
peaceful and filled with joy. You feel grateful for and content with
the simple things. A common example of what happens when we
don't have clarity is lack of boundaries. We all have a friend who
will put up with anything from the person he's dating, and that
happens because our friend doesn't know what he wants out of
that relationship. He lacks clarity, and therefore lacks boundaries.
But the real issue is that people who live like this are living from
a place of fear. Our friend is afraid that if he stops putting up with
shit from the woman he's dating, she'll leave him. Then he'll be
by himself forever and die alone. I chose this example because
we've all heard it from a friend or two over the years, and because
the fear such people have is palpable. It's so easy to find yourself
in a place like that, living scared, when you lack confidence and
clarity.

To draw your own path to Beautiful Money, it's imperative to
start figuring out where you want to go, what your destination is.
Many of us stay in the same money zone and see stagnant growth
in our businesses and incomes because we are afraid to get out of
our comfort zones and try new ways. We all get weighted down in
our lives. It takes courage to fully recognize when this happens,
and then to own it and break free. It takes courage to say no to
people, to disappoint people, and to give up people-pleasing. It
takes courage to choose leadership over passive living. It takes
courage to stand up for yourself and to live in total alignment with
your true voice and greatest desires.

When we don't take these actions, we tend to let our fears keep
us from possibilities—we settle for "living small." We let other
people design and dictate our lives. Think about it: Who is in the
driver's seat in your life? Your boss? Your partner? Your friends?
Your colleagues? Your busy-being-busy schedule?

When we want to accomplish everything, we are not focused

on anything. Research has shown that we can't multitask and accomplish two goals at once, no matter how hard we convince ourselves we can.

Creating focus and clarity about what you want your life to look like five years from now will help you figure out what to accomplish tomorrow. I once worked with a client who wanted to be certified to teach yoga, complete a nutrition course, be a vice president at her company, start her own business, be in perfect health, and get her MBA. She also wanted to travel the world and have a family. She set a two-to-three-year goal for herself to accomplish all that. The lack of clarity in her plan was obvious. She didn't know what to do that afternoon because she wanted to get everything done at once, which is impossible. She couldn't even manage her time, much less everything else that was happening in her life. She was a hot mess. Over the years I have also realized that everyone has their own journey and my role is not to interfere. Sometimes, we need to experience stress, overwhelm, and chaos.

But creating a clear intention for the future, which we'll do later on this week, makes it easier for us to align our daily habits and behaviors with what we want our end result to be. Without clarity and intention, we don't have boundaries, a clear path, or enough space in our mind-set and life to change and create abundance.

PRINCIPLE SIX: BALANCE ACTION AND ALLOWING

We should always be in the driver's seat in our lives, but sometimes we need to take our hands off the wheel and let the universe steer. Figuring out when to take control and when to take a step back is both an art and a science.

This principle is still my greatest teacher. I tend to overvalue action. I am such a big believer that greatness results from being a person of action that it still feels uncomfortable for me to sit back and allow. This discomfort is common among overachievers.

We don't know how to relax and be comfortable in stillness. For me, meditation and yoga help. I have also found that walking meditations work really well as a starting point for busy beings like me.

In 2014 I decided to start a new work project and spent most of my days trying to *make* it a success. I had a one-and-a-half-year-old at the time and was pregnant with my second child. Instead of resting, and enjoying my life and my pregnancy, I let my old overdrive habits kick in at full gear. I had the ability to take as much time off as I wanted, to embrace motherhood and pregnancy. Instead, I would consistently sacrifice family time to work on my project. I was busy being busy. I was rushing, forcing, and trying too hard. This resulted in a disagreement with my colleague that spiraled into a legal dispute and in turn delayed the project's completion.

There were a million little signs that I wasn't balanced in terms of action and allowing and was out of flow, but I ignored everything. Intuitively, I knew I should take a break, but the type A in me wanted to finish the project, to check items off my to-do list, to accomplish my goals *no matter what*. I spent a year in action—and did about zero allowing, which is a big reason why the project ended up stalling out. I saw the signs but bulldozed my way forward anyway. I made a common mistake: I didn't listen to my heart or my gut.

The definition of "action" is pretty obvious: it's the work we do, what we put in motion, literally the actions we take. Action is the key to turning knowledge into wisdom. And like I always say, "Knowledge is nice but wisdom is *hot*." On the flip side, "allowing" is letting the universe work on your behalf. Allowing is when you feel flow. You might associate this with feeling fully in your groove, when the concept of time seems to warp and you feel like you could keep doing what you're doing forever. Both taking action and being in a state of allowing are important.

We should strive for a balance. If we've been taking action, we need to recognize when it's appropriate to take a step back and allow. Similarly, we need to learn how to recognize when we're being called to make a move, when we need to shift gears and create! A great guide is our emotional state—how do we feel in the moment? When you feel that burning in your belly, that tingling feeling (which often keeps you up at night with excitement and inspiration), it's time to act! A creative energy is flowing through your body and wants to manifest. It's time to move!

However, if we're always in action—something I still fall victim to—we tend to live in the mind too much and lose connection with our body, spirit, and the world around us. Spending too much time in our own brain can cause anxiety, anger, and depression, as well as negative self-talk and a tendency to attack ourselves for every little thing we can't control or that goes wrong. That's when we fall victim to our fears. We think, "If I can just get this project done," even though we know that pushing ahead is not aligned with what we truly want, that it's creating more stress and even making us unhappy. Even so, we want to check that project off our to-do list, dammit! Our fears might say, "If you don't stay busy, your business and your life are going to fall apart." This is a symptom of disconnection with the rest of ourselves.

What we need to realize is that checking off a box on our to-do list is an empty accomplishment. If we rush the journey, without feeling connected to it with our whole selves, just in order to accomplish a goal, we're not celebrating that journey. We're exhausted and frustrated. Our tissues are filled with tension. All we can think is, What's next?

Most of us live in a constant state of action. If you've been totally busting your butt and begin to feel negative or burned out, that's a sign that it's time to step back and allow. Another great example is when we suddenly get sick with a cold or flu out of nowhere, and it totally takes us out. That's a physical signal from our body that we need a time-out from taking action. There will always be a day when you hit a wall in terms of energy and flow—

that's your body signaling you to slow down and take a day off. That's what this principle is about.

Learning when to flip the switch between action and allowing can be difficult, but it's key to creating Beautiful Money. We must learn to connect our minds with our hearts and recognize that our hearts are so much smarter than our brains. (Later on, in Week Two, I'll provide some tools and exercises that can help you become more mindful.)

PRINCIPLE SEVEN: GIVE MORE, TEACH MORE, BE MORE

When we're in a place where we want more from life, especially when we want more money and success, we tend to ask questions like "Why don't I make more money?" or "Why don't I have what she has?" or "How come I don't live in a house like that?" or "Why did he get that promotion instead of me?" We may think, "I deserve to have more because I work my ass off!" But we don't realize that we're making ourselves a victim.

In order to make positive change, especially when we want to create financial and holistic abundance, we need to stop seeing ourselves as a victim of circumstances and to start acting from a position of leadership. We need to say, "Okay. I want a promotion. How can I show my boss and management that I'm ready for a bigger role at my company?" Or, on a personal level, "Okay, I want more friends. How can I be a better friend to the people I'm close with?" It really all comes down to the simple philosophy of prioritizing serving over selfishness. Asking yourself, "How can I be of service to the planet today?" will instantly shift your awareness from getting to giving. I find that when I need a little external influence to help me get out of a selfish funk, beautiful music helps me shift to a place of generosity and giving, sometimes almost instantly. I also love to hang out with people I have a deep admiration for. These people don't waste time gossiping, being jealous and selfish. They shine bright, authentic, and vibrant life on planet Earth. They make me a better person. My dear and close friends—you know who you are!

We need to be leaders in our own lives. If we want more, we have to serve more. If we want to advance in our career, maybe mentoring someone is a way to show the universe (and our boss) that we're ready for a promotion. If we want more friends, being a good friend to the people we're already friends with is a great first step to broadening our social circle. And on the days when you are feeling a little down, a little selfish, and a little competitive, go help someone successful achieve one of her goals (even if she has a much bigger tribe and business than you). Go help her make her dreams happen! There is something small but significant you can do for her. Go do it!

At the end of the day, this principle is about showing up with excellence each day and making sure we are acting from a perspective of being in control of what happens to us, not the other way around. This principle helps us heal and avoid what I call "excusitis." You can be either a person who prioritizes results or one who makes excuses. Because you can't do both. People who live inspiring, purposeful, and aligned lives don't have the time or space for excuses. And neither do people who want to create Beautiful Money.

When I help clients learn how to "be more," I always ask the following questions: Do you feel a deep connection with yourself and the world around you? Do you feel like you are holding back in your life (and where)? What would you do if you knew you could not fail? Who are you not helping because that person happens to be more successful than you? What are you not doing because of fear? Do you feel grateful for your life (not in your head but in your heart)?

A huge component to creating Beautiful Money is to give when we don't feel like giving. Giving back to the world can be as simple as overdelivering to a business client or spending time with a friend who would really benefit from your full attention. When we live above our own dramas and problems (in other words, out of the trenches), we are contributing to the world from a much higher place. Just being more present and connected each day is a gift to the world. When I catch myself living small or in my own drama, I remind myself how little that does to move my own life or global healing forward. With a subtle shift in thinking, I can get myself out of my head and into my heart.

Universal law states that when you give, you receive—and so we should all strive to be generous each and every day, with our time, our money, even our thoughts. The rule to remember is: the more we give, the more we receive, and the more gracefully we receive.

PRINCIPLE EIGHT: LEAD WITH SOUL, LEAD BY EXAMPLE

As I mentioned before, knowledge is nice but wisdom is *hot*. I'm inspired by people who live what they teach, who walk the talk, who truly strive to have a life that's aligned with their purpose and values—so I aim to do the same. Just before I quit my corporate job, I went on a road trip to meet my dear friend Sophie.

When I got to her new cottage in the country, I was completely blown away. Sophie was wearing yoga pants, a beautiful tunic, and a scarf but looked incredibly chic. Her hair wasn't done and she wasn't wearing any makeup, but her skin was glowing as if a makeup artist had dropped by earlier in the morning and applied the perfect bronzer. She was deliciously radiant and had total freedom. Sophie had just purchased her cozy country dream cottage and had filled her spacious office with vision boards and inspirational mantras. She had a yoga mat right next to her desk so she could practice and meditate throughout the day. Once we both settled in, she told me all about how she had grown her own business from the ground up. At one point in her story, I stopped her and said, "I don't care what you're doing, but sign me up!"

We can all be Sophie for the people we love. We all know from experience in the world that lots of people are unhappily chasing success without fulfillment, so there's an opportunity for us to show our friends, family, and community that there's another way. By living the Beautiful Money principles, we can step into leading others simply by demonstrating that it *is* possible to carve your own path, to be fulfilled and still create more wealth and abundance than ever before. We can truly lead by example. There is so much beauty in simplicity and in soul-centered living. This is the authentic path and the path to Beautiful Money.

In order to carve our own unique, idiosyncratic path to Beautiful Money, we need to know where to begin. Evaluating your starting place is what we'll tackle next, in step two.

STEP TWO: THE POWER OF NOW

The second step to creating Beautiful Money is to lovingly get honest with yourself about your life and your finances. One of my greatest mentors taught me that an important step to creating wealth is to get crystal clear about where you are today. A common pattern I have seen with clients over the years is a deep fear of facing their current money landscape. The mere thought of having to total up all their debts and liabilities on one sheet of paper evokes complete tension in their bodies. It's easier to be ignorant of how much debt you've accumulated over the years. A lot of people make the conscious decision to remain unconscious of their finances.

But what most people fail to realize is that a clear starting point makes all the difference when it comes to building wealth. Taking a loving, gentle approach to facing the numbers, with both head and heart engaged, is the most powerful, positive, and healthy step to changing our relationship with money. By providing ourselves with a complete yet honest view of where we're at—and doing it without judgment—we let the universe know that we're ready for change.

Facing your finances head-on may be intimidating, especially if you've been avoiding looking at your bank accounts for some time. Trust me, I've been there. But I also know how empowering it can be to get a clear picture of where you are at right now. It's how you can harness the power of the present. After all, there is a reason why it feels right to be on the path to Beautiful Money in this very moment. There's a purpose you have to find.

As your mentor and guide to creating holistic wealth, I would like to remind you that from minute to minute you are exactly where you are supposed to be. Every day, every hour, every second of our lives has value. That's because time is the only thing we can never get back. We can earn more money, buy more stuff, and make new relationships with people. But once time has passed, there's no way to recapture the moments, the days, the years that we weren't present for. However, once we begin to live more consciously, we realize how vital time is.

Beautiful Money will help you be more present in your life, but first we need to figure out what has been holding you back from wealth and abundance. This step is the beginning of that process. The greatest gift you can give yourself at this point in the program is a current, comprehensive, truthful view of your finances. In this step, I'll help you compile all your financial information in one place. We'll examine your net worth, how much scarcity and abundance is present in your life right now, and your current credit score. We'll also take a look at where you are in terms of producing prosperity and what you're spending your money on, so you can begin to target areas for growth.

I like to think of this step as a gentle yet empowering wake-up call. The objective isn't to place blame or to feel bad about ourselves; instead, we want to evaluate our starting place without judgment, fear, or beating ourselves up for what's happened in the past. This may be challenging. But I encourage you to avoid focusing on the mistakes of the past. Instead, think about the leaps and bounds you are about to make toward your goal of holistic wealth. The more compassion and love you treat yourself with, the easier moving forward will be. I cannot stress enough the importance of being gentle, loving, and kind to yourself. If your net worth is in a negative state right now, love yourself even more. If you realize that you owe more than you earn, take a deep breath and actively be kind. Remember that we are not focusing on the past, on what might have gone wrong or what reasons may have created a less than fruitful financial landscape. Today we are getting clear about our money numbers—without judgment. There is no space for blame, second-guessing, toxic energy, or being hard on ourselves for what happened in the past.

Try to keep calm while you crunch your numbers. It's time to get clear, not critical. Think of it as inhaling courage and exhaling judgment. Create some emotional space and allow it to permeate your body to make room for the abundance, the love, and all the greatness that's on the way.

Beautiful Money Tip

*I*F EXAMINING YOUR finances makes you feel completely freaked out, try surrounding yourself with things that make you feel happy and relaxed. Perhaps you can calculate your net worth to your favorite song or create a blissful environment for yourself before starting. Get yourself some yummy natural candles and some green tea. Create a peaceful ambience in your office or room before doing this exercise. Add some music and lovingly remember that you are on time and on track!

Now is the time to get clear and excited about all that's to come. If you're uncomfortable physically, you'll be uncomfortable mentally and emotionally as well. Tackling a challenge in a positive atmosphere correlates to a more positive mind-set, which means that you'll be able to feel more understanding, forgiving, and empathetic toward yourself and your financial state. If you find yourself being hard on yourself as you reveal your numbers, call that fabulous friend who always makes you smile.

Your homework will be to discipline your mind as you calculate and to practice not judging yourself. And always remember (regardless of the numbers) that every day is a new day, and this just might be the day that turns your life around!

Whether you're feeling good about your financial health or worrying that your net worth will literally be negative, emotions will surface. That's normal and to be expected. The point of this course is to observe those feelings without attachment, so you can start on a new path of money mindfulness that will lead you to more holistic wealth and abundance than ever before. This takes practice and patience, but you will get better and better at it over time!

Our brains are wired to roll with comfort, security, and repetition. We don't spend much time thinking about why we do what we do, whether it's making coffee in the morning, buying things we don't really need, or making the minimum contribution to retirement savings. Similarly, we don't realize that our habitual behavior when it comes to money is about more than just ourselves. When we talk about finances, we're also talking about the values we grew up with and how our parents handled money, as well as our own financial history. That can be a lot of baggage to pick through and let go of. Being mindful of your feelings will help you detach from what you may have been carrying with you for years, if not your whole life.

By paying close attention to ourselves and being present in our emotions every single day as we work through this process, we allow ourselves to move on. We will no longer blindly follow the same patterns and behaviors and beliefs that have brought us to the point where we want to change. Instead, we can use our newly found mindfulness to change our behavior on a daily basis, and focus instead on the Beautiful Money we want to create.

We'll discuss how to reshape our money beliefs and patterns later on, but right now I want you to concentrate on observation. Notice how and what you're feeling as you follow the exercises in this step. Whatever comes up, take good notes, and practice not attaching any value to those thoughts and feelings. This is known as meditative thinking—allowing your thoughts and emotions to pass like a cloud in the sky. Let the emotions flow through you, and allow those emotions and judgments to pass without deciding they're the whole truth. (With practice, you will get really good at this!)

When we stop attaching meaning to negative feelings like anxiety and stress, the discomfort these emotions cause passes too. By committing 100 percent to pursuing a new path of holistic wealth, we allow the thoughts and behaviors that have been holding us back to disappear. Instead, we feel light and energetic and optimistic about the journey *and* the destination.

In order to reach that positive place, we need to create clarity. Within this step there are five exercises: three that are entirely objective and two that are subjective. We'll begin with an objective exercise: requesting your FICO score.

GIVE YOURSELF CREDIT

Credit is crucial when it comes to creating holistic wealth, because it creates financial leverage. There are three reputable agencies that you should check: Equifax, TransUnion, and Experian. Each report is a little different, but according to federal law in the United States, individuals can receive a complimentary report from each of these agencies once a year. Sites like Annual Credit Report.com offer these reports free of charge.

It's important to check your credit report on an annual basis for discrepancies and accounts that you may have forgotten about. For instance, my husband and I use credit cards only when we have to, usually for travel and big purchases. We go through our credit card and banking statements every week, line by line, in order to make sure that all the charges are accurate. A few months ago, I spotted three transactions that seemed fraudulent. It wasn't a ton of money, but I called the credit card company right away. We discovered that Ric's credit card number had been compromised on a previous trip, and we were refunded the money right away.

It's amazing what you will uncover if you check your credit card statements regularly, and the same applies for your credit in general. But most people rarely make sure their credit report is accurate. According to an article in *USA Today*, 65 percent of Americans don't check their credit reports annually.[2] This might seem like no big deal, but a few unnecessary or incorrect dings on your score could affect the interest rates you pay on loans, how much money you can borrow in the future, and sometimes even whether or not you can rent an apartment.

So, what's a good credit score? According to NerdWallet, FICO scores range from 350 to 850.[3] Although each lender or bank differs on what is a "good" score, the general guidelines are these:

Bad credit: 300–629

Average credit: 630–89

Good credit: 690–719

Excellent credit: 720 and up

If your credit score is lower than you expected, breathe. It's easy to improve your score by being more mindful of what affects your credit.

The number one rule when it comes to credit is to *pay your bills on time*. This might seem obvious, but it's easy to miss a payment in the hustle and bustle of life. Automate payments if you can— most banks today have a "bill pay" feature that you can set and forget. I like to pay my bills as soon as they come in. This is a simple habit that makes me feel light and empowered.

Second, *keep credit card balances at no more than 20 percent of your limit*. Having high balances on your credit cards can lower your credit score because lenders assume that you cannot repay the balances you've already accumulated. For example, if you have a credit card with a ten-thousand-dollar limit that always has a nine-thousand-dollar balance, lenders assume that you are charging more than you earn. However, if that same card has only a thousand-dollar balance, lenders will be eager to offer you a higher credit limit, hoping that you'll spend money so they can earn more interest from your business.

Third, *manage a few with excellence*. Review all your credit card accounts to see what cards you actually use, what cards have the lowest APR, and what cards you could possibly pay off. Having only a few credit cards makes it easy to manage those accounts closely.

I like to keep things as simple as possible, so for the longest time I had only one credit card. It was my rule, because managing a single credit card is so easy! But recently I changed my personal rule to having two credit cards. It's easier with four children and traveling a lot internationally to have options. I didn't feel comfortable traveling internationally with a family of six and only one credit card. What would happen if we lost that card? So I just added a second credit card and use it as an emergency card. As I mentioned earlier, it's a great idea to review all your transactions on a weekly basis, which becomes very time consuming when you've got multiple credit cards, store cards, gas cards, reward cards, etc.

Make it simple, and keep it that way. If you do decide to cancel a card, make sure to get confirmation in writing that your account has been closed. Often people see canceled accounts listed as "open" on their credit reports. It's much easier to dispute these types of discrepancies when you have a written letter from the lender or credit card company.

Fourth, *limit how often your credit is checked.* Your credit score decreases every time your credit is checked by a third party—for anything, big or small. Ever applied for a store credit card because it got you a discount on that day's purchase? Ding. Applied for a job or an apartment? Ding. They may seem innocuous, but these kinds of small dings on your credit can really add up over time when you're not conscious of it.

Finally, *build a credit history.* The reason I had only one credit card for so long was because I was so afraid of accumulating debt. But what I came to realize is that I had zero credit history because I never let banks loan me anything! It's important to build a credit history over time, whether by taking out an auto loan or a mortgage, by opening up a credit card for frequent-flier miles, or by paying your utility bills with a credit card and then paying it off every month. If your spouse or partner takes care of the money, building a credit history can be tough because you're not the one paying the bills. But it's important to build your own credit. Don't put yourself in a situation where you don't work your money muscle daily. Being in the passenger seat when it comes to any area of your life will make you feel less in control and could negatively impact your self-confidence. So if your partner manages the money, offer to pay for the utilities or the cable or something else that crops up every month in order to build your own independent credit history. It's good for your finances and your self-esteem. Even if you have a wealthy partner, build your own credit history!

ATTRACTING ABUNDANCE

Beautiful Money flows toward us when we are acting from a positive and powerful place, when we believe we are worthy of it. But a lot of us unknowingly live our lives from a place of fear and scarcity. We might think we're generally optimistic or that we lead by example or make healthy choices, when in reality fear drives most of our decisions.

Think about your life. Do you keep your job because you love it or because you are afraid you won't be able to land your dream job? Do you stay with your partner because you unconditionally and madly love him or her or because you're afraid to be alone? Do you live with the idea that unless you hustle every day, you might lose everything? Do you people-please because you are afraid of not being liked?

On page 39 is the Beautiful Money Abundance Scale. This is meant as a subjective tool to show you how emotions guide you through each day and in general throughout your entire life. We all move back and forth along the scale. Ideally, we want to exist mostly on the abundance side. But many people either make extreme swings back and forth or find themselves stuck in a scarcity mind-set.

One of my mentors says that people tend to live like thermometers, running dramatically up and down on the scale throughout the day. What I like to teach my clients is the idea of being a thermostat instead. Thermostats have developed an ability to discipline their thoughts to hold relatively steady throughout the day. Their emotions aren't as volatile. Their mood may vary a little, but usually not a lot. That's because a thermostatic approach to our emotions is one controlled from within. It's very similar to how a thermostat works in our homes to regulate and control temperature. The goal is to create a steady environment, and the same applies for us.

In contrast, when we live unconsciously, as thermometers, the environment determines how hot or cool the mood is. We live each day as if we don't have control, and we have no idea how to regulate our own inner temperature. That creates a mentally and emotionally exhausting existence, which is usually filled with drama. Life becomes an emotional roller-coaster ride. However, our goal with Beautiful Money is to live more temperately. We want to fluctuate between the two sides of the scale less frequently and less drastically. We want to live like thermostats, not thermometers.

So how do we know where we land on the scale? When we mostly live from a place of fear, and a place of "I'm not good enough," it's easy to burn ourselves out at work because we're always afraid our career will somehow falter if we don't stay late at the office or work on every project possible. Deep down, this comes from a fear that we won't have enough money or that people won't like or accept us if we aren't behaving the way we're "supposed" to. We might be afraid to be alone or to break out of conformity. There are millions of consequences we could be afraid of, and these fears inform our choices about nearly every aspect of our lives, including money.

How do you know when you're living from scarcity? It doesn't necessarily mean that you are totally broke. I know plenty of people who have lived in an abundant state despite not having a ton of cash. I also know plenty of people who have lots of money but don't live in abundance mentally, emotionally, or spiritually. The key to Beautiful Money abundance is living prosperously, harmoniously, and gratefully. To discover whether you lead your life from a place of fearful scarcity or one of Beautiful Money abundance is to tune in to how you feel. Are you happy or are you angry? Do you feel hard and tense or soft and open?

Beautiful Money Tip

FOR ME, A major aha moment was when I realized that I was living from a place of fear. Deep down, I was afraid of not being liked and not having enough. I was a professional people pleaser! Making this discovery was intimidating and really rocked my world. After some soul searching, I realized that the people I truly admire are loving, kind, authentic, and open but also clear and confident. They are not afraid to gracefully disappoint people or say no to things that don't align with their greater vision. My yoga practice, along with my Beautiful Money practice, keeps me aligned and abundant. Yoga is a perfect partner for the Beautiful Money program!

If you don't already do yoga, consider adding a class once or twice a week while you're doing the program. Combining the exercises in this book with the mindfulness and body awareness you'll learn and practice in a yoga class will put you on the fast track to transformation and greatness. Dance is also a fabulous complement to the Beautiful Money program. Fluid movement helps to unleash stale energy and release issues from the tissues. Whatever your preferred method, I would encourage you to complement your Beautiful Money program with daily movement. Moving your body while you are learning will help you drop the knowledge right into your body. It will help you get more connected to the information and speed up the rate at which you apply the knowledge and wisdom from this book to your life.

When it comes to money specifically, often what I see is that people are afraid that they won't have enough. That's what leads to the constant sense of chasing I described in the introduction. We accomplish one goal, take the teeniest moment to celebrate it, maybe, and then move on to the next thing—we're always chasing some benchmark that keeps getting further and further away. That cycle keeps us locked into behaving out of fear. I have worked with students who have plenty of money but feel that no matter how much is in their bank account it's never enough. The fear of not having enough money, ever, is why so many of us endlessly chase money. The solution to overcoming our fears is clarity.

This exercise will help you get clear right here, right now. Take a pause and breathe in deeply. Exhale. Look at the scale and let your emotions indicate where you land on the spectrum. Remember: try not to judge where you are—just observe.

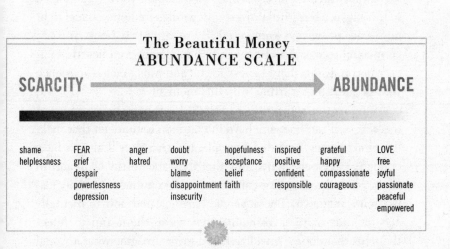

The Beautiful Money
ABUNDANCE SCALE

SCARCITY ➜ **ABUNDANCE**

shame	FEAR	anger	doubt	hopefulness	inspired	grateful	LOVE
helplessness	grief	hatred	worry	acceptance	positive	happy	free
	despair		blame	belief	confident	compassionate	joyful
	powerlessness		disappointment	faith	responsible	courageous	passionate
	depression		insecurity				peaceful
							empowered

When we live in a state of fear, our actions are not in alignment with our true selves. We feel negative. In contrast, when we live in a state of abundance, we feel confident about meeting our needs and trust that we are exactly where we are supposed to be.

Gauge how you are feeling in this moment. Where are you right now? Where would you like to be? Are you living from a place of anger or joy, stress or confidence, frustration or empathy? Do you feel totally overwhelmed by this exercise? Do you feel like you are not good enough? Or do you feel encouraged by where you are now?

The point of this exercise is to observe where we exist today, in this very moment. We need to be mindful that many factors will cause us to move around on the scale. We are not robots, and our lives have contrast. What we want to do is to build our mental and emotional muscles to align with thoughts and feelings of love, connection, joy, and abundance. It might not be realistic to believe that we can feel 100 percent abundance all the time, but I believe it is in the realm of possibility. We are worthy of belonging, being loved, and being good enough. We are absolutely worthy of Beautiful Money. We deserve the very best! You are worth it! You deserve it! My greatest desire is that you will know you are connected to this big and beautiful universe. Regardless of how you feel right now, you are always connected. By reading this book, you are connected to me. And I am sending my loving and heartfelt energy to you. Know that I believe in you and want you to experience your greatest life, starting from this moment.

Many of the successful experts I have had the pleasure of meeting and interviewing have in common a mind-set that making more money is always possible and that they'll always have enough. They believe not only that they are worthy of Beautiful Money but also that they can create it on command. Scarcity just isn't on their radar. These people have learned how to mentally accept and invite in thoughts that serve them and to reject thoughts that don't align with their destiny. Imagine what it would feel like to live this way. Open your heart and mind to how different your days would be. Adopting a hopeful mind-set requires us to fully open our hearts and be vulnerable every day.

Creating each day from a place of unconditional love and faith is what I strive for. I believe there will always be enough and that abundance is always possible. But sometimes even I struggle to act from a place of faith instead of fear. I occasionally fall victim to scarcity thinking, but I shift out of it much faster than I used to. Awareness is the key. I just don't like how scarcity thinking makes me feel. When I don't feel abundant and joyful, I practice giving and gratitude. It isn't always easy to feel grateful and giving when I'm frustrated or disappointed, but I am aware that this is my life lesson. Like everyone, I'm a work in progress.

Later on, I'll share practical tools to help you rewire your brain so it's easier to stop living from a place of fear. But for now we want to practice believing that it's possible to live every day from a place of love and abundance. Let's remind ourselves that we deserve to spend our time on this earth peacefully, lovingly, and powerfully. Our time here is short but we can make our legacy long.

WHAT'S YOUR (FINANCIAL) WORTH?

Before we get into the numbers, I want to reiterate that feeling worthy of wealth is fundamental to creating Beautiful Money. If we don't feel worthy, wealth simply cannot make its way to us. I like to call it "wealth worth." And our first step to creating healthy wealth worth is to create a clear picture of where we're starting out from. We need to discover and clarify where we are right now in our lives, so we can move forward with greatness, confidence, and purpose. We need to calculate our individual net worth. Remember that our goal here is to create clarity. Be honest and real but not emotionally attached. This is no time to be hard on yourself. It's not time to judge yourself or curse yourself. This is where your self-love work is put into practice. Love yourself regardless of your current reality. Make space for that love. Clarity helps us get ready for the change and greatness that awaits. Focus your attention and energy on the beauty you desire and the Beautiful Money that is on its way to you.

I like to think about my net worth as my annual leadership report card. I tell my clients to calculate their net worth every year, because it can bring insight as to how powerfully, confidently, and creatively they are living. Comparing your net worth from year to year can tell you a lot about yourself—not just how much money you have. Part of Beautiful Money is to focus on growing our net worth each year, not to make more money, but because increasing that number requires us to change and grow as people.

Whatever net worth you may have in mind as an ideal, it is already out there, just sitting pretty, waiting for you to find it. Our goal right now with Beautiful Money is to identify our current financial landscape so we have a starting point. Once we have done this, we will focus all our attention and energy on the creative process and our destination.

To me, the true gift of creating wealth isn't about money. It's about the strength and leadership we develop along the path to creating Beautiful Money. It's also about the possibilities and doors that open to us once we have created it, as well as along the way. Creating Beautiful Money will require discipline, honesty, vulnerability, courage, and a loving commitment to ourselves—the certainty that we are worthy of wealth and that we deserve the best in this lifetime.

Beautiful Money Tip

EVERY COUPLE HAS its own way of handling joint and separate finances. However, if you are married and/or living with your partner, I recommend calculating your net worth both individually and as a couple to get a clear picture of where you're at. (This is true even if your spouse is not participating in your Beautiful Money journey.)

When calculating your individual net worth, do your best to divide joint assets so each partner is accountable for his or her own assets and liabilities. This will give you clarity on both your individual finances and the overall financial state of your union. Similarly, strive, when creating financial goals, to create individual goals that benefit both of you. For instance, if one of your goals is to travel more, perhaps both partners can contribute to a savings account specifically dedicated to an annual trip.

The Beautiful Money Net Worth Calculator

This tool is meant to provide an estimate of your overall net worth. If you prefer a more detailed assessment, I recommend speaking to a financial professional such as a certified financial planner (www.letsmakeaplan.org).

ASSETS – LIABILITIES = NET WORTH

Assets include:

Cash on hand (savings accounts, checking accounts, CDs, money-market funds)

Retirement accounts (401(k), IRA, SEP)

Stocks and stock funds

Bonds and bond funds

Variable annuities

The value of your primary residence

Land or real estate

Value of a business you own (we won't get complicated with calculating business values, but your business may be an asset if you can sell it or even a part of it)

The value of your car

Art, collectibles, jewelry, and furnishings that could be sold

Liabilities include:

Mortgages

Car loans

Student loans

Private loans

Credit card balances

Lines of credit

Outstanding debt (such as taxes owed)

Don't freak out if you have a negative score! This happens a lot with my clients because of student loans, mortgages, and other forms of debt. As the personal finance blog *Simple Dollar* advises, it's important to remember that "every time you make one of those debts smaller or one of those assets larger, your net worth will increase. So, you can increase your net worth by paying off your debts, saving and investing money, and reducing your spending."[4] Which is exactly what we'll do in the Beautiful Money program!

As I mentioned before, it's crucial that we look at our net worth without judgment, knowing that the number on the page is simply a starting place. I do recommend spending time with a financial expert to help you calculate a more accurate and detailed net worth, but you can use your own calculation as a great and simple starting point.

MAKE GORGEOUS SPACE 45

ARE YOU READY FOR PROSPERITY?

What is powerful about the Beautiful Money program is that we will carve out the time to examine the habits, behaviors, and beliefs we have around money so we can get rid of the ones that no longer serve us. This will create fabulous room for prosperity, holistic wealth, and greater abundance. The quantitative analysis of our financial health must be a priority, but we must also take a qualitative look at our money landscape.

A terrific measure of our emotional and mental starting place is the Beautiful Money Prosperity Scorecard. I encourage you to complete this scorecard at the end of each week as you proceed through the Beautiful Money program. Comparing your results from week to week, you'll literally be able to see how much you've changed. Your answers this week are simply a starting point. You wouldn't be reading this book if prosperity and wealth had already arrived, but I promise—they're waiting for you. Remember that we are lovingly keeping score here, so there's no need to be hard on ourselves or judge what we may have done in the past. As we begin to move forward, we harmoniously graduate to a higher Beautiful Money frequency.

The Beautiful Money
PROSPERITY SCORECARD

If a sentence rings true, mark it with a check ☑

☐ Throughout my day, my thoughts are creative, abundant, positive, and grateful.

❑ I write down my goals with clarity, commitment, soul, and emotion.

❑ I take daily action toward achieving my goals. I discipline myself daily to maintain focus and consistency.

❑ I give more than I ask in return. I exceed expectations by underpromising and overdelivering. I aspire to serve as many beings around the globe as possible. I always lift up those around me.

❑ I quiet my ego and open my heart as I manifest my greatest desires. Self-care, self-esteem, and self-love are my greatest priorities. I aspire to judge less, compare myself less, while softening more into my divine essence. Each day, I remain flexible, open, and loving.

❑ I am self-motivated. Although I reach out to other people and ask for help and guidance, I live from the driver's seat. I wake up each morning with a renewed and inspired inner force that pulls me toward greatness.

❑ I flow more and force less. Each day, I recognize that my emotions tell me how aligned I am (or am not). I take time each day in solitude to listen to my body and my soul. I trust that the universe has my back and that great gifts are making their way to me.

❑ My net worth increases every day. I am an excellent money manager. If I am not already debt-free, I am closer and closer every day. I focus my cre-

ative energy on creating more cash flow and mini-
mizing unnecessary or unwanted expenses. I
aspire to learn something new about money every
day.

❏ Each day, I commit to results and not excuses. I
choose where my energy goes.

BEING MINDFUL OF DOLLARS AND CENTS

If you feel discouraged at this point in the process, that's completely normal. Remember, you bought this book because you
know deep down that a change, even an evolution, in how you
think about and handle money is necessary now. It's time to commit yourself 100 percent to the Beautiful Money journey and to
start putting the theories and principles you've read about thus far
into action.

Tracking our daily spending is a great way to truly evaluate
what's working for us and what is not from a holistic perspective.
The previous exercises in this step provided a broad overview of
what has kept you from abundance and wealth. The next step is
to pinpoint the source of what's held you back emotionally and
financially. Whether the cause is stress, debt, or stress caused by
debt, we can act with more awareness if we can be specific about
what no longer serves us.

Tracking our money for a week provides yet another completely
objective perspective on our finances. It can help us pinpoint
where we're spending money unnecessarily and create greater
clarity about what's truly important to us.

The Beautiful Money
DOLLAR TRACKER

FOR ONE WEEK, track every dime you spend. And I mean every dime! Expenses, fun money, what you take out of the ATM, bank fees, what you spend on your kids, what you spend on food—everything. Ask for receipts, and double-check them against your accounts online. Take a ledger or a notebook and write down every transaction, both from receipts and in your accounts—including automatic transfers, payments, and subscriptions.

Once you've got your list, I want you to start another list on a separate sheet of paper. Divide the sheet into three columns: "Expenses," "Needs," and "Wants." As a general rule, expenses are things that you can't just stop paying, like student loans or a mortgage. Needs vary, but school supplies and clothes for your children, groceries, and personal care products like soap and paper towels fall into this category for most people. Wants are stuff that's not necessary. For some people, wants are the reason for debt (e.g., a better cell phone or a new pair of Louboutins). Buying clothes you don't need, spending mindlessly on things, going out to dinner or ordering takeout when you could just as easily cook, buying extra toys for your kids—I could go on and on. Today online subscriptions can be an expense or need that quickly turns into a want because we rarely cancel these services when we no longer utilize them. Some colleagues I know spend hundreds of dollars on software or on marketing tool subscriptions that just sit on their computer. Expenses like these are true expenses when you use the services for a specific purpose, but they quickly become wants when you just mindlessly spend money on them without even noticing it. (And this is easy to do when the payments are automatically deducted from your account!)

When you categorize a transaction, use your intuition. Expenses tend to be obvious, but the line between needs and wants can be blurry. For instance, if organic food is a must for you, the extra cost of buying those groceries should be classified as a need, not a want. Housing is a need but it can be a want if you've chosen to live in a fancy apartment that's more expensive than you can afford. Your body will absolutely give you signals about what category your spending falls into. Listen to your inner voice and ask it to help guide you. You absolutely know the difference between a need and a want! Even in times of tight cash flow, I have always prioritized healthy food and wellness activities. These are absolute needs for me. I would rather stop all clothing shopping and restaurant spending. I would feel absolutely misaligned if I negotiated my values and moved well-being into the want category. Health is your greatest asset (and your business card!).

I would advise revisiting the dollar tracker every six months or so to make sure you're still on track. That said, if you're the type of person for whom mindless spending is an issue, part of your Beautiful Money journey should be tracking spending each and every week.

This first week is all about making space and creating clarity. By giving ourselves a new perspective on our finances—both objectively and subjectively—we bring awareness to patterns, beliefs, and behaviors that may have flown under the radar. This begins to create clarity.

Next we will cleanse ourselves of what no longer serves us—and by doing so will open up gorgeous space so Beautiful Money can begin to flow.

STEP THREE:
THE BEAUTIFUL MONEY CLEANSE

I could actually spend this entire book teaching you how to cleanse and clear for prosperity. I am a chronic cleanser. This week has been all about creating clarity, and the Beautiful Money Cleanse gracefully wraps up your very first week of the program and positions you for greatness in the weeks to come. I'm a huge advocate of balancing action and allowing (Beautiful Money principle six), but to truly move forward it's absolutely crucial to get rid of what's not serving us. With time, this will become a daily practice! Mental and physical clutter in our environment—at home, at work, in our hearts, in our thoughts—creates disorganization, which by its very nature keeps us from being focused and clear. My friends and family know that I am a bit obsessed with cleansing (with intention, of course!). Clutter clogs up my creativity, my cells, my mind, my tissues, and my being. Feeling free, spacious, and open has become my top priority. When I feel free and spacious, I feel like I can take on the world and serve my highest potential. I promise you will grow to be a little positively obsessed with cleansing too!

I have been known to give away clothing, furniture, cars (well, one car to date), and things in my life that have served me well but are ready to move on. I like to keep things circulating. Things that have brought me joy should be passed along to put a smile on the faces of others. On a daily basis, I practice nonattachment to stuff. As long as I feel peaceful, aligned, and in a space of giving, I am happy. When things get cluttered or my environment gets messy, I feel drained and yucky.

Have you ever felt like this? You are a giving and generous person but because of mess and chaos in your life, you feel as if you are draining the world of precious energy and resources. When I feel like this, it's time for a shift! It's time to graduate to the next level of greatness and prosperity. It's time to joyfully embrace the Beautiful Money Cleanse. Get rid of the shit that is holding you back, weighing you down, and keeping you from graduating to your next life class.

At this point, you might think: Leanne, my house is totally organized and neat. My office is immaculate. But I would ask: What about your to-do list? What about your day planner? Your car? Your body? Your emotions? Your in-box? What about your pantry and your closet? What part of your life is oozing chaos and just being busy? Are you loaded with guilt and heavy emotions that weigh you down? Do you carry excess emotional fat? I believe cleansing is both an inside and outside job. Clearing space for the beauty you desire starts with your physical environment but also includes your internal landscape (body, mind, and emotions).

Clutter is not just about having too many trinkets and knick-knacks around your home. In my opinion, clutter can be physical, emotional, and mental. Usually, it doesn't show up physically first. Clutter typically builds up mentally and emotionally before it barfs all over the physical environment. Clutter can be guilt and stress associated with being a people pleaser. Clutter can be physical—like having a bunch of clothes in your closet that you never wear or a ton of junk food in your cabinets. Clutter can be ninety e-mails in your in-box before noon every day. Clutter can be an unhealthy or toxic relationship. Clutter can be spending way too much of your precious life force on things that just don't matter. Clutter develops every single time yes comes out of your mouth when you really want to say no. Clutter can be developing the habit of overpromising at work, which can make you feel over-whelmed in other areas of your life.

And what does clutter feel like? If you really tune in to your body, it feels like you have a brick in your belly. It weighs you down and holds you back from that beautiful, radiant, and delicious feeling of lightness. When I did my first Beautiful Money Cleanse, I was holding so much unhealthy emotional energy and fear in my body that when I got rid of all the clutter that was no longer serving me, I physically lost five pounds. Taking the scary step of cleansing my stuff helped my body to cleanse from within.

Remember, what creates beautiful music are the spaces between the notes. To truly thrive, we need mental and physical space as well as lightness in our lives. We need a chance to take a step back and truly appreciate the good we have been given and the great that is on the way. We need time in our lives to plan, to pause, to appreciate, and to be fully present. We need to make space to feel truly alive.

We need to create that space and distance in our own lives, and the Beautiful Money Cleanse will help you do exactly that. This is a highlight for me when I teach the course, both online and in person, because it always makes a huge shift in my clients' perspective.

The Beautiful Money CLEANSE

THE PURPOSE OF this exercise is to

- Help you *detach* from what doesn't matter
- Make *space* for the great
- Allow you to *breathe*
- *Lighten* your emotional and mental load
- Create a sense of *flow* in your environment
- *Let go* of negativity and everything that no longer serves you

I'm not going to sugarcoat it: the Beautiful Money Cleanse is a challenge for most of my clients. Most of us have been primed to believe that our material possessions correlate to our value as people. The more stuff we have, the more successful we are. Deep down we might know that's not true, but getting rid of the things we think define who we are can be difficult. Personally, I love cleansing because it gives me the opportunity to practice detachment. But it can be an uphill climb, especially if you're not used to cleansing or have been stuck in your routine for a while.

The Beautiful Money Cleanse is intended to be holistic. You are in the driver's seat and can decide how extreme or how subtle you'd like this exercise to be. Some easy ways to start would be to clear your closet of clothes and shoes that don't make you feel amazing. Donate or sell whatever is in good condition. I like to go through my medicine cabinet and get rid of beauty products that have expired or that I simply don't use anymore. You'd be amazed at how much space that creates! I regularly donate and give away my clothes. Remember, you're making space for the beauty you desire.

After you've taken some baby steps, examine your internal life. Is there a behavior you used to love that today needs to go? Are there thoughts or beliefs that no longer serve you? Negative people who used to be close friends or family but now aren't so supportive? These are all aspects of life to consider when cleansing. Maybe you need a break from social media. Perhaps a detox from your in-box over a weekend, when checking e-mail really isn't necessary, will help clear your mind.

Challenge yourself to cleanse on as many levels as possible. The more effectively you cleanse, the more space and change you'll create. Like many things in life, the amount of effort and thought you put into the cleanse directly affects the results you'll see. Consider making Sunday your weekly cleanse day, and watch your world transform.

The Beautiful Money
CLEANSE CHECKLIST

HERE ARE SOME ideas to get you started:

- Clothing, shoes, and accessories you don't love
- Beauty products that aren't healthy and nontoxic
- Toxic, unhealthy, expired, and processed food
- Harmful cleaning products
- Books, magazines, and paper clutter (junk mail, anyone?)
- Messes (in your car, office, home, outdoors)
- Clutter (anywhere—physical, mental, or emotional)
- TV time
- Negative language (about yourself, other people, and situations)
- Overpromising or overscheduling yourself ("I'll-do-it-itis")
- Gossip and drama (feel the vibration gossip makes in your body—yuck!)
- Technology and electronics
- Toys and kids' stuff
- Property (furniture, cars, boats—anything you no longer use or need)
- E-mail in-box (personal and work)
- Unhealthy relationships
- Storage (stuff in your home that you never really need)
- Dust-bunny boxes (you know you have some)
- Other shit that weighs you down and blocks your energy flow

There are two important aspects of the Beautiful Money Cleanse that aren't on the checklist. First, I'd like you to identify what you are trying to control in your life. Are you trying to control a loved one? Are you struggling for control at work? Where in your life are you micromanaging?

For example, some of my clients tend to obsess over what their spouses are doing, what their kids are up to, or how productive their subordinates are being, on a moment-by-moment basis. But most of that time is wasted, because what other people do is out of our control. All that time could be used more productively—whether it's to make space for you to be creative, to give yourself a much-needed break, or simply to practice detachment and observing the emotions around why you are trying so hard to control. Energetically, this brings us back to the abundance scale. What you are responsible for is your own journey and being the best you can possibly be. As a mom, I practice this philosophy daily. I am responsible for the well-being and safety of my children but not for diminishing or hindering their ability to develop their own wisdom. Their bodies might be little but they are my teachers. I learn from them daily and don't trick myself into believing that I am in charge. I am guiding them on their own unique path but not interfering by imposing my own judgments, projections, and beliefs. I believe in my children and trust that they have great wisdom.

When we try to control someone or something, we are acting from a place of fear. We're scared that if we let go, something will fall apart instead. We don't trust that everything will be fine if we're not constantly on guard. We grip too hard on someone else's problem and, by making it our problem, hold ourselves back. Not to mention that micromanaging tends to create stress, drama, and a lot of emotional crap for everyone involved. Having faith in the world around us and trusting that the universe has our back is a helpful practice. Seeing everything as a great adventure and learning experience is a helpful place to start. We are all students and teachers in this lifetime. Some of us forget to be students, and some of us forget that we have much to teach!

Beautiful Money Tip

*I*F YOU JOKINGLY label yourself (or others label you) a type A or a control freak, make a list of everything and everyone you worry about or try to control. This could be as simple as cleaning up after your spouse every time there's a mess in your home or fretting about your friend's new boyfriend. Once you have a list—and it may be quite lengthy—ask yourself: What am I trying to prevent in this situation? What am I afraid of? If you are honest with yourself, those two questions will typically explain why you're so freaked out about losing control.

You can also ask yourself what would happen if you let go and surrendered to the idea of not having control. (Here's a hint: you would likely soar!) The illusion is that control creates success, but the truth is that it's probably holding you back from your next level of absolute greatness! Letting go of control will result in more radiant beauty and a state of well-being and lightness unlike anything you have ever experienced.

Consider trying a new approach by asking yourself where you are gripping or striving for control, and then embracing the philosophy that if you let go, the universe will guide you toward your destiny.

The funny thing about control is that it's an illusion. Typically, we want to control aspects of our lives that we are afraid will spiral out of control if we're not actively managing them. But what if it's the opposite?

A great example is micromanaging family finances. Usually, for those of us who are coupled up or married, one partner manages the money most of the time. And that's not usually a problem, especially when both partners have input and make decisions together. However, when one partner has exclusive control over the purse strings or restricts the other person's spending, deep down there usually isn't enough trust between both partners when it comes to money. It's easy to imagine how that uncertainty can reverberate throughout the relationship and cause problems in other areas. That being said, if the controlling partner begins to let the other person participate in the decision making when it comes to their mutual finances, it helps to repair trust between the partners and can increase both partners' self-esteem and actually create a little empire for the family overall. I've seen it happen—not just with money but with housework and parenting as well.

Figuring out how to let go of what we are trying to control is Beautiful Money principle six, balancing action and allowing, in real life. When we try to control, control, control, we are in a constant state of forcing. To create clarity, we need to let go and allow the universe to do its work. By getting to the root of *why* we want to control, we can be more mindful and consciously let other people's problems be just that—their problems, not ours.

The second component of the Beautiful Money Cleanse that isn't on the checklist is a physical cleanse for your body. If we want to clear as much space for abundance as possible, we need to consider everything in our lives, from the big stuff like what's causing us to feel stressed or trapped to the tiniest cells in our bodies. Human beings aren't one-dimensional. What we eat affects how we think and how we feel. How well we take care of our bodies directly correlates to our perspective on the world around us. If someone has a chaotic lifestyle, a crazy messed-up bank account, and a negative circle of influence, it's likely that body experiences stress at a cellular level too. Chronic inflammation, fatigue, autoimmune reactions like allergies and asthma, feeling burned out all the time—these are all symptoms of clutter in the body's ecosystem.

The Beautiful Money Cleanse is intentionally *holistic* because we need to recognize singularity—the concept of oneness that unites body, mind, and spirit. We are made up of trillions of cells, and those cells desire to feel clean, light, and free of chaos. Cleansing our environment will only go so far. If we want amazing results from the outside world, we need to start making changes on the inside too. When we make cleansing our body as much of a daily practice as cleansing other areas of our life, the results become exponential.

Years ago, when I was a carb and sugar addict, I made it a practice to clear my pantry of anything processed, sugar filled, or unhealthy. It was a simple task that started me on the path to feeling healthier. Once in a while, an unhealthy food would make its way back into the pantry, but it never stayed very long. The simple, regular habit of cleansing my pantry made me feel like I was prioritizing myself—and that, in turn, made me feel even more amazing. One of my toughest addictions was Diet Coke. After working through the principles of the Beautiful Money course, I was finally able to kick the habit. Once you have cleared and cleansed your life and your body, your cells will speak to you. They will tell you how they feel with every sip and every bite. You will choose radiance and vibrancy over tongue teasers! You will desire to feel as free and light as possible, every moment of every day. You will choose to feel truly alive.

Beautiful Money Tip

HERE ARE FIFTEEN quick and easy tips I give my clients when teaching the Beautiful Money course.

1. Drink water with lemon upon waking (if you can drink hot water with lemon, even better). This gently wakes up your digestive system and is soothing too.

2. Give yourself a smooch (on the hand, arm, or wherever feels right) and say, "I love you." If this is new for you, it might feel a little uncomfortable at first. Remember that your cells hear you and will awaken with vibrancy to the words "I love you."

3. Soak in a Himalayan salt bath for twenty minutes every day or two (I buy one that has lavender in it!). In my experience, this is great for releasing both physical and emotional toxins from the body.

4. Buy organic essential oils to create a relaxing environment (these can be used in laundry, baths, cleaning, and on the body).

5. Buy fresh flowers. They bring beautiful energy and happiness into your home.

6. Create a clean, super-Zen environment to boost mental clarity and creativity.

7. Limit or avoid caffeine (except for green tea).

8. Fill your diet mainly with fruits, veggies, seeds, nuts, and healthy fats.

9. Drink juice daily (especially green juice).

10. Start a daily supplement program to help your cells thrive.

11. Drink herbal teas (chamomile and vanilla are my favorites).

12. Carve out at least thirty minutes each day for creative time.

13. Move daily (minimum of thirty minutes).

14. Meditate for at least five minutes in the morning and before bed. This will bring great order and peace to your life.

15. Choose natural cleaning, personal care, and food products to remove toxins and chemicals from your body.

Cleansing inside and out will create tremendous space in your life. Soon you'll start to notice a shift in how you perceive and act in the world on a daily basis. Clearing the shit that's simply not working anymore gives the spirit a huge boost and creates amazing clarity. Try it for yourself and you'll see.

MAKE ROOM FOR THE GREAT

DURING THE BEAUTIFUL Money Cleanse, I challenge you to examine every aspect of your life. It can be tough to figure out what's working and what's not—especially if you are surrounded by stuff, ideas, and people that no longer serve you.

This exercise is big and juicy and cathartic.

Make a list of every activity and task in your life that you do out of obligation, that you really don't like, that you resent, that you never want to do, or that causes feelings of tension, frustration, anger, or resentment.

I become frustrated when I spend time on trivial and unimportant tasks for others. I am a recovering people pleaser. I used to say yes to almost everything and everyone (even if my body was screaming no). I used to say, "Sure, I'll take care of it," but then I would get stuck in a pile of busywork that made me want to quit life and move to some faraway island where no one could ever ask me for a favor again. The heavy tension in my body, associated with decades of people-pleasing, left me unhappy, angry, and frustrated. I realized that I was deeply afraid of not being liked and (what I have recently discovered) of being alone. I had to relearn how to behave and how to respond. I had to train myself how to gracefully let people down. I had to learn that even if I say no, I will still be loved. This has been my toughest lesson and my greatest teacher. I had to rewire my brain (which wasn't always pretty). I had to set boundaries, evaluate friendships, and make a loving and nonnegotiable commitment to myself. I had to learn how to love myself through the process of saying no and disappointing people. I had to learn to get comfortable with it. I joke that "when I used to be nice" I would do those things for people. I am still nice but am more mindful of how I want to feel and serve. I have committed to being a bright and loving light on a global level. This keeps me from committing to unhealthy activities and things that won't bring me joy. Getting bogged down in trivial shit that doesn't matter or serve the world (or me) became toxic to my being. Over time, I realized that I never learned to set healthy boundaries for myself—and I couldn't exactly ask other people to respect boundaries that didn't exist. It took many emotional breakdowns for me to understand that only I was responsible for the frustration and anger that built up in my body. And I became so ready to let that go. I became absolutely ready for my next chapter in life. For that to happen, clear boundaries had to be established. So I am still nice—but now I have set boundaries, gracefully clear.

Once you have your list, really sit with it. Most of us are so out of sync with ourselves that we truly don't know who we are or what we want from our lives. This unbalance can become physically heavy in the body, creating even more tension and negativity. Not having clarity can eventually make us feel like one day we're going to snap and scream out loud, lose our patience completely, or, worst of all, just give up.

To create Beautiful Money, we need to move away from that kind of negative thinking and move toward a more positive and inspiring perspective. Compiling and evaluating the list of what isn't serving us is a great step forward, but it's equally important that we are ready to take action and implement some new habits that will lift us up a vibrational notch or two.

A few years ago, I worked with a client named Alex who was frustrated because she felt like she had two jobs: one at work and one at home, as her family's housekeeper. Alex told me that because she worked at home, her husband seemed to expect her to have time to clean up after him, to cook meals every night, and basically to be a housewife—all while running her own business. "I don't think he realizes that I work all day too," she said to me. "He leaves a messy house in the morning and comes home to a clean house with a pot on the stove at night. What does he think I do all day? Does he think I have a magic wand to cook, clean, and do my work simultaneously?" Over time, Alex admitted, she had come to resent her husband. I recommended that she tell him exactly how she was feeling, so she did. Her husband, Matt, was shocked.

"I don't know what I thought," he told her. "But I guess I figured you had the time." Of course Alex didn't have the time! By figuring out what was at the root of her frustration, though, she was able to cleanse her schedule of the perception that Matt expected her to cook and clean. This is just one small example, but by doing this exercise you should be able to shed some light on what's holding you back from the life you desire.

Challenge yourself this week with the Beautiful Money Cleanse, but there's no need to go overboard. When I first ditched my own crazy corporate-burnout lifestyle, I decided to sell everything I owned, but most people don't have to go that far. My husband and I love adventure and love a fresh, clean start. We like to do a big cleanse every seven years or so. We have both sold everything in our lives a few times, in order to start new. It is very freeing but less than practical! Go with what works for you. We are gypsies at heart and feel a need to fully cleanse when we feel tied down. This isn't something I would recommend unless you know yourself really well and can handle it. It can be overwhelming, so don't make an impulsive decision to cleanse your entire life. Start small and see how it feels.

The purpose of Beautiful Money is to detach from the things that hold us back and realign our values in order to move forward. A big component of that is to untangle identity and self-worth from material possessions. Life is not static. Practicing nonattachment is remembering that things come and go in life. Sometimes we'll have a ton of cash, and other times we'll have to be more frugal. Sometimes we'll be in a positive mind-set, and other times we will have to rein in our negativity. We all have good and bad days—I'm afraid that's not going to change for anyone. But we can learn to ride the wave when it comes, and anticipate what's on the way when we're in the midst of a swell.

However, when we begin to believe that there will always be enough, we no longer grip things so tightly. We don't need to be overly attached to money, because we can always make more. When we get too attached to stuff, we worry about what will happen if we don't have it. We begin to attach our own value as people to material things, which over time erodes our confidence in our innate ability to thrive on our own.

Practicing Beautiful Money is about creating an abundant life. In order to do that, we have to know deep down that there will always be enough, and that life is constantly changing. We're going to have periods when money is tight and periods when money is abundant, but if we are able to detach from what happens on a minute, day-to-day level, we can begin to see the bigger picture.

Learning how to detach can be difficult at first, because everything in Western society encourages us to entwine our identities with material things. But consider this essential truth: the only thing we can't get back is time. If we lose money, we can earn more. If we lose our house, we can find another home to live in. If we lose a partner, there's always the possibility that we will fall in love again. If we lose a job, we can apply for another one. But if we waste time, it's gone. Just gone. And time goes by so fast.

The ups and downs of life happen to everyone. When we are able to practice detachment by trusting that the universe has our back and is looking out for us, and that we will never truly be without, we can begin to have a healthier level of attachment in our lives. This is what ultimately makes the Beautiful Money Cleanse empowering, not scary or threatening.

Beautiful Money Tip

*P*EOPLE TEND TO freeze when faced with a holistic cleanse, because it can be hard to figure out where to start. I love to begin by clearing out my closet, but something else might appeal to you—like spring cleaning your home, eliminating clutter in your office, or simply taking out the trash and getting rid of your children's unused toys.

I find that my clients can usually locate, in the back of their mind, one particular area that has been ripe for a cleanse for a while. If that rings true, the area that's been bugging you is exactly where you should start. It may be the closet or it may be that your car is a disaster. But there's usually *something* the universe has been nudging you to cleanse, and that's the best place to start. If you are beginning to feel fearful about approaching that area of your life, it's okay to start small. It's also okay to ask for help.

That said, this exercise has no timetable and should be done at your pace. The ideal place for you to be while cleansing is at the edge of your comfort zone. A little tension and anxiety is to be expected. But I also advise my clients to take a break if they start to feel completely overwhelmed or so nervous that they might throw up. This can be hard work, but I promise it's worth the effort.

For many of my clients, other people are a huge source of mental and emotional crap. If demands from people at work or expectations from friends and family are on your list of spurs for negative emotions, take a break. Delete your in-box. Ignore social media. Turn off notifications on your smartphone or, better yet, turn it off completely for a few hours. (Or for as long as you can stand it!) The fact that we're constantly connected can create very dense, negative energy that makes us feel on edge and anxious. When we're always anticipating the next notification, it's hard to be present.

If this sounds like you, put away all technology for a few hours to see if you can begin to cleanse yourself of other people's drama. Empty your in-box and shut down social media notifications. If something is truly important, your friends and coworkers will contact you again.

Similarly, this is a great opportunity to truly consider whom you're spending time with, especially those in your inner circle of influence. If you have a friend or family member who doesn't lift you up, make you feel good about yourself, or contribute equally to your relationship, stop hemorrhaging your energy and time.

Toxic relationships make us feel trapped, insecure, and dependent on others for validation. Feeling like you have to tread cautiously, please a friend in exchange for his or her approval, or live small is never worth it. Your time and energy are more valuable than that.

THE BEAUTIFUL MONEY PRACTICE

Creating abundance is constant and fluid, just like life. Like mindfulness, yoga, and meditation, the practice is its own reward.

I've found that this program tends to work better if we think of Beautiful Money as its own daily practice as well.

The Beautiful Money practice has eight components, which help us to become more self-aware, to know our feelings and mental state, so we can be more mindful and practice detachment on a daily basis. Combined with the Beautiful Money principles, these components create a practical framework for us to make change, create clarity, and begin on the path to holistic abundance and wellness.

Breathe Deeply

If you start to pay attention to your breathing, you'll be amazed at how often you hold your breath when you're tense or stressed. It can be helpful to take a few deep, cleansing breaths (in the nose and out the mouth) when you have a tough day or encounter a stressful situation.

Start and End Each Day with Five Minutes of Seated Silence or Meditation

Sit in silence. No tech, no sounds. Turn off your brain and just observe what happens, without judgment. Let thoughts pass by like clouds in the sky. Set aside ten minutes for yourself every day. You'll be amazed at how much a simple break can change your mind.

Let Go of Fear, Worry, Judgment, and Tension

When we are able to acknowledge fear, worry, judgment, and tension, we can root out their sources and clear them from our lives—reducing negativity and making more space for abundance.

Be Open and Flexible

What we resist persists. Recognizing where we have rigid beliefs and behaviors, and learning how to soften in those areas, makes us better equipped to handle what we can't control in our lives (most everything).

Nourish Your Body, Mind, and Soul with Life and Love

Focus on feeding your body and mind well. Be conscious of the link between what you eat, what you think, and how you feel.

Love Yourself and Those Around You

A client gave me a fortune cookie a few years ago that simply read, "You deserve the best." It's been on my computer monitor ever since as a reminder to never settle. If we don't treat ourselves with kindness, compassion, and positive energy, we are doing a disservice to the world.

Flow More, Force Less

Where can we allow the universe to do its work? This is all about awareness. I have a daily practice in which I check in with myself to see if I am flowing through life or forcing. I can tell that I'm beginning to force in areas of my life when my body feels off or tense.

My practice is to use breathing, meditation, and yoga techniques to help me soften, let go, and return to a state of flow. Writing this book was a perfect example of flow. Nothing felt forced or pushed. Contrast is very helpful when you are learning to flow more. Your body remembers how you felt the last time you may have forced too much to make money, to complete a project, or to please someone. Compare that to how graceful and peaceful your body feels when you are in perfect flow.

When we feel like we are getting out of sync, it's important to do what we can to ease our body back into a flow state. Practice yoga, breathing, or meditation or simply move your body more to expel that junky, forced energy.

Be Thankful for All You Have and All That's on Its Way

Gratitude is the gift that never stops giving and allows us to believe that the universe eternally has our best interests in mind and will provide us with all we need to thrive.

By incorporating the Beautiful Money practice in your everyday life, you'll not only become more mindful and self-aware but also exponentially increase the clarity and space you've created during this first week. When it comes to holistic abundance, simpler is always better—and more joyful.

WEEK TWO

Your Beautiful Mind

*L*AST WEEK, WE created space for true beauty. As we lighten our load—physically, mentally, and emotionally—letting go of baggage and the other clutter that's held us back from abundance, we signal that we are ready for the extraordinary. Over the past week, we let go of whatever is no longer serving our greatest potential. But before we can truly benefit from the clarity we've created, we need to flex the greatest muscle we have: our mind.

Henry Ford once said, "Whether you think you can, or you think you can't—you're right."[5] Thoughts are immensely powerful, yet very few people are aware of the control and influence our self-talk can have on our lives. When we don't lovingly focus on the things we truly desire, our minds can cause all kinds of chaos and drama in our lives.

Our mental muscles are mysterious yet miraculous tools for creating positive, wealthy, and joyful lives. We just need to learn, through consistent training and practice, how to use the power of the mind to create better results for ourselves. Here are some simple questions to help you determine whether you are successfully flexing your mental muscles (and, if not, areas in which you can improve). Ask yourself if you are:

- Living on purpose
- Committed to pursuing your dreams
- Crystal clear about what you are creating
- Feeling focused and aligned in daily life
- Living drama-free
- Open to inspiration and ideas
- Focusing attention on what you want, and not what you don't
- Living each day productively outside your comfort zone
- Making your dreams happen
- Seeing your goals and dreams as already done, achieved, destined
- Not letting the opinions of others distract you from your dreams

During Week Two, we will discuss how our minds set sail for what we create but our emotions are truly the key to everything! A daily practice of focusing our attention on the thoughts that bring us closer to what we want in our lives is essential. Our thoughts affect how we feel, and we all know how that can turn out. For example, think of the last time you woke up feeling frustrated or angry. It's easy to let negative thoughts set the tone for your entire day and to find yourself in a downward emotional spiral.

I used to have a habit of letting the way I started my day drive the entire day. Before I recognized that I was in the driver's seat, I would let myself fall victim to my thinking. Food is a perfect example. If I started my day with unhealthy food choices (like chocolate), I would surrender the entire day to feelings of despair.

I would commit to an entire day of eating unhealthily and being extremely hard on myself. It wasn't about food; it was about my mind! My thoughts at 8:00 a.m. would set the tone for the entire day. If I slipped once, I would give myself permission to sabotage the entire day. I didn't realize that this pattern was keeping me far away from living happily and abundantly.

What most people don't realize is that the brain, where all our thoughts originate, can be strengthened like any other muscle in the body. With constant practice and patience, we can train ourselves to focus on the positive and motivating thoughts that align with what we want. We can also learn to toss away thoughts that make us feel frustrated, angry, envious, jealous, and broke. Like any great endeavor, this takes practice, persistence, patience, and discipline. Every day is a new day and a new opportunity to strengthen our mind to the next level of joy and abundance.

Week Two is about figuring out what we value most and how we should shape our lives and our mind-set to create more abundance. If you're like most of the people I work with, you've come to Beautiful Money because you crave a lifestyle that's more in line with what matters to you. But before you can achieve that, we need to figure out what your ideal lifestyle is. Would you like more love in your life? Do you desire more peace and freedom? Are you aching to be more independent with your work? Do you want to make time with family your top priority?

Maybe you're more like me when I first started this journey: deeply craving a lifestyle that is alarm-clock-free and filled with time and freedom.

To experience a lifestyle that's aligned with and authentic to who we are, we need to figure out what we value most. We also need to gain the confidence to step out of the herd and into a place of leadership, and to change the way we perceive and think about ourselves and the world around us. This is obviously no small task. It's a deep and beautiful commitment, but it must be nonnegotiable if you desire a fulfilling and extraordinary life.

This week I'll help you figure out what you truly want—and, even more important, how to shift the way you think. I'll share tools that help you broaden your worldview and foster confidence in yourself. Doing something different from what most others are doing can be a challenge. Most of us need help to break out of the herd mind-set, to free ourselves from living in scarcity, chasing success, fearing money, and worrying about what other people think.

Many authors, including Napoleon Hill and Earl Nightingale, have taught me the importance of making decisions based on my own desires, and not on pleasing others. So many people make choices based on what others want or expect and on what will maximize their chances of fitting in.

As a recovering people pleaser who lived for years making choices to accommodate and please others, I know how important it is to focus on the intention behind each decision I make. I ask myself if my decision is based on love or on fear; if it is authentically based on love, then I courageously move forward. I occasionally slip back into people-pleasing and inauthentic decision making, but this has become a rarity. This practice of identifying the intention behind my decisions has created so much more emotional freedom and happiness in my life and is a cornerstone of Beautiful Money.

It's easy to see how acting for others can cause us to be out of alignment with our own interests, beliefs, and desires. We want to act and live consciously and powerfully so the self-fulfilling prophecy and similar behavioral biases don't have as much influence over our lives. This begins with taking control of our thoughts—the root of all our behavior.

We can create Beautiful Money only when we live in a way that's aligned with what we value most. That requires us to harness the power of our thoughts and bring what happens in our heads closer to our hearts. We need to step out of the socially driven, unconscious way we've been living our lives. Instead, we should create and define rules and expectations for ourselves. We must develop our own personal philosophies about how we want to live our lives. By doing so, we create freedom—not just financial freedom, though that's totally a goal and a benefit of the program, but temporal and emotional freedom too.

Deciding to live consciously requires understanding the influences of our internal and external worlds. This week, I'll show how changing the way we perceive our thoughts and self-talk can increase confidence and change our results, allowing us to force less and flow more.

STEP ONE:
FIND OUT WHY

I strongly agree with Mel Robbins that the new F-bomb is the word "fine." In today's world there is an epidemic of people settling for a "fine" lifestyle. (As mentioned, Mel Robbins talks more about this idea in her amazing TEDx talk, "How to Stop Screwing Yourself Over."[6]) Every single day I talk to people who hate their jobs, who dread Monday, and who resent their bosses and coworkers. I've even spoken to some who have purposely gotten pregnant in order to stay at home with the kids instead of go to an office they hate. Both at work and at home, there is literally an epidemic of people who spend their days not doing *anything* they truly love. It's also not uncommon to hear people carving into their friends, gossiping about their supposed favorite people, and complaining regularly about their partner or spouse. Does this sound extraordinary and aligned to you? It doesn't to me.

So how do we fall into the trap of settling for being just "fine"? Well, it's easy because settling for fine absolves us of any responsibility for our own unhappiness. It's easy to settle for fine because it's just good enough. It's easy to settle for fine because it allows us to blame the world around us. It's easy to settle for fine because we can develop a million excuses for why we're not where we planned or dreamed we'd be. It's easy to settle for fine because it's more comfortable to complain. It's easy to settle for fine because we fit in with everybody else who has settled too. *But when it comes to Beautiful Money, fine isn't good enough. It's not even close.*

This week is all about creating change in how we perceive the world around us. To do that, we have to define for ourselves what is important. It is incredibly easy to end up in a place where fine is acceptable, where we are making money at the expense of our time, our family, our soul, our joy. It's easy to create a lifestyle focused on external success that is completely void of happiness and fulfillment. Hello, that's how I spent my twenties! But when we're ready to make a change, it's important to realize that we have to step out of our comfort zone and leave fine behind.

The first breakthrough that takes us past being just fine happens when we clearly define what truly matters most to us. To gain positive and healthy momentum in our lives, we must stop focusing on what we don't want and stop doing the shit we hate. When we begin to focus on what we want instead of what we don't, momentum builds and we begin to experience transformation. For lasting transformation to occur, we must learn to let go of what is no longer serving us. I don't mean just mentally let go; we must learn to let go of any shard of energy that might be hanging around in our bodies and energetic space. We must learn to fully surrender anything that is part of our past but should not be part of our present. This could include language that isn't serving us, people who aren't healthy for us, habits that are harmful, or simply putting others' needs and desires before our own.

When we put into practice the idea of giving up the good to make room for what is great, motivation is felt and transformation occurs. In a very real sense, this moves us from living in a state of being just fine to knowing that holistic wealth is on its way.

YOUR FOUR PILLARS

I had an interesting conversation with my colleague Emma a few years ago. She said to me, "Leanne, I love my job but something feels off. I'm not exactly miserable, but I'm not truly happy either." This is one example of the fine state. I asked Emma what she liked about the job. She said she enjoyed the work itself but hated how much she had to travel. "With two little kids," she said, "I really want to spend as much time as possible with my family."

An objective of Beautiful Money is to create income in a way that is aligned with who we are as individuals and what's most important in our lives. Hating our jobs or how we make money is a signal that our work conflicts with what we value the most. Everything might look great from the outside—maybe you have a prominent position, maybe you have a flashy title, maybe you travel around the globe, maybe you have a pretty corner office with a great skyline view—but inside, you just don't feel quite right.

That is a signal that your core values—what I call the "four pillars"—aren't aligned with how you make money. You might like the work, as Emma did, but not the position or the company you work for or the circumstances. Or perhaps, like me, you need to change everything about your career path. A position or a career might be great, but if it's not aligned with what's most important to you, then it is not sustainable.

Here's why: no matter how much money you may make, having a job or an income stream that conflicts with your core values is never going to make you feel satisfied, happy, or fulfilled. And if how you make money conflicts with what's fundamentally true for you as an individual, you will never be able to create wealth. That's why, no matter what the salary, a job that is not aligned with any or all of your pillars is unsustainable in the long term.

To create Beautiful Money, we need to flip the usual script. We need to align what we value most with the way we generate income. This next exercise is awesome because it will help you dig into what you really value in your life.

WHAT ARE YOUR FOUR PILLARS?

WHEN WE DESIGN our lives around what's most important to us, it's easy to flow and live authentically. Start by answering these two questions:

*When you feel negative, resentful, and stressed,
    what's the cause?*
*What makes you feel happy, light, fulfilled, positive,
    and energetic?*

Typically, your answers help shed light on what's most important to you.

For me, answering the first question helped me realize that family is a core value, because I feel unhappy when I'm not present for friends and family. On the flip side, I realized that happiness and joy for me stems from having autonomy—the ability to do what I want, when I want, without someone else dictating how I spend my time. Combining these answers, I came up with freedom as another core value.

While doing this exercise, feel free to create a list of the four pillars that are most precious to you. This is your very own, personal list of the four core values that are most true for you. When you neglect these values, you might look happy and successful on the outside but inside you feel like a fraud. When you neglect these four most precious pillars of your life, you feel grumpy, frustrated, unhappy, stressed, and generally out of alignment. Without these values in your life on a daily basis, you are living small, not living up to your potential, and feeling merely fine instead of amazing.

It's time for you to create your four pillars. Here are some examples for inspiration:

Health	Honesty
Family	Success
Freedom	Community
Autonomy	Service
Learning	Safety
Leadership	Openness
Community	Philanthropy
Mindfulness or	Faith
presence	Global living
Connection	Wisdom
Integrity	Vitality
Peace	

Beautiful Money Tip

'VE FOUND THAT a key to reducing stress is to

1. identify your four pillars, and
2. prioritize those activities in your life.

This isn't always easy but you can start small. Begin with a baby step. If one of your pillars is health or wellness, you might start doing a quick workout during your lunch hour. I practice a forty-minute workout regimen that works great for me, with three babies at home. That forty minutes helps me reconnect and realign my body, mind, and spirit.

Balance might not always be possible, but clearly identifying your four pillars will help you quickly prioritize activities in your life and bring you a much greater sense of joy and fulfillment. I look forward to these workouts in a way I never did when I would spend ninety minutes on a treadmill. But keep in mind that any baby step toward a life that's aligned with your core values is good. Perhaps your baby step is to designate one night of the week as a date night with your honey. Your baby step could be to visit the local farmers market with your family every Saturday morning instead of watching cartoons. Making small changes consistently over time is what truly creates big transformation. You can't do it all, but you can get really great at prioritizing the activities that fuel your mind, body, and soul.

Our core values are our fundamental pillars. These words represent what is most precious and important to us in our lives. Consider them part of your lifestyle DNA. We can use these core values, moving forward, to figure out whether an activity or action is aligned with what we truly want from life. For example, I love yoga. As a certified practitioner, I'm tempted every so often to open my own studio. However, one of my core values is freedom. I know that being tied to a physical place where I have to show up and manage people every day would make me feel constrained, so I have to resist the urge. (Of course, I'm not saying others would feel restricted owning a yoga studio. I just know that I would feel that way eventually. When I really dig deep into my heart, I feel most free and happy just being a student of yoga and taking a class every chance I get. But everyone is different. I am still open to the possibility of opening, in the future, hopefully in a tropical location, a yoga studio that doesn't require me to physically show up or manage the day-to-day!)

Knowing your core values is crucial because it can help you avoid opportunities today that will make you feel out of alignment tomorrow. This is a great example of saying no to the good so you can say yes to the great. Once you begin practicing and living Beautiful Money, there will always be opportunities because you are a vibrant, positive soul who attracts both the good and the great. What's important is to take the time to gauge how the opportunity *feels*. Is it exciting? Or are you already sort of dreading it?

Beautiful Money Tip

WHEN IT COMES to choosing which opportunities to take and which to let pass, money or financial wealth shouldn't take the lead in your decision making. It may seem counterintuitive to let a lucrative opportunity pass, but if you're not excited about a particular project or job, and it goes against your intuitive truth, there's not enough money in the world to make it worth your effort and time.

Making Beautiful Money requires you to lead with heart and intuition when making decisions. Cash flow, returns on investments, and wealth creation are absolutely important, but not at the expense of your health and your soul. Take a moment to register your initial gut feeling when decision making is required. What I do know is that when people choose money first, they often experience negative (even harmful) side effects, including frustration, unhappiness, resentment, anger, anxiety, stress, exhaustion, adrenal fatigue, and even despair. Don't believe me? Try it out.

If an opportunity is not aligned with what matters most to you (your core values), let it pass. The opportunities that don't make your soul sing, or that you can't be excited about, just end up taking space where a better opportunity could be. Don't settle for something fine—wait for something great!

When we practice judging our decisions by how we feel, and identify what our core values are, making decisions becomes much easier. If we know that health is a core value, we know that we *must* prioritize the activities that help us feel healthy. We must prioritize our day and our week so that well-being activities take the top spot. This can be tough at times if we have a busy career or commute to work.

Prioritizing ourselves does take planning, but it's necessary. When we don't make time for the activities that fulfill us and reflect our core values, we become unhappy and unsatisfied, and we begin to accumulate tension and anger. Even if we just take twenty minutes of our day to work out or ten minutes for a guided meditation, that time must be nonnegotiable. When we don't put ourselves first, when we don't take care of ourselves, we do a disservice to the world around us. The world needs us to shine as our brightest and most authentic selves. If we fail to do this, how can we create a lasting legacy? How can we live without regret if we don't fully experience life as our greatest selves? If a core value is family, perhaps we mark every Saturday or Sunday, or a few of the hours after work, as family time. A dear friend of mine has a movie night every Friday with her husband and kids. Their Friday nights are nonnegotiable. After sustaining this tradition for years, their family is connected, aligned, and happy. That same friend also has a date night with her husband every Sunday, when they have a glass of wine and just hang out. I admire my friend dearly, and she has been such a great mentor for me. Her core values are clear—family, health, freedom, and integrity—and her schedule reflects that.

Beautiful Money Tip

*L*OOK AT YOUR calendar for the next eight weeks. Pick one or two activities that are totally aligned with your core values. Whether it's meditation in the morning, time with your kids at night, or just a yoga class that you love but never seem to get to, block off that time in your calendar so that it's nonnegotiable. This simple act will make you feel happier, because you're putting yourself first—and will help you practice living in alignment with what you value most.

It isn't that hard to see why our society is overwhelmed, broken, and stressed out. The majority of time is spent on things that don't restore us or add value to our lives; it is spent on activities that are not aligned with any of our core values. This is where I got tripped up in my twenties (a lesson that I cherish and that made me who I am today). During that period of my life, I spent 90 percent of my time doing things that didn't matter: pleasing others, chasing a promotion, commuting, eating in my car or on the go, sitting in front of my computer, spending money on things that didn't matter, answering my phone and e-mails all day long. I prioritized pleasing others over living an authentic and fulfilling life for me. Often I see people choose to spend their time on activities or work that are sort of in line with their core values—like me opening a yoga studio, since I love teaching. Although I love yoga, I would much prefer to have it be a time for me to breathe, move my body, and connect with myself. At the end of the class, I can go home without any responsibility. I am an ultraresponsible being, but my yoga practice is my time to let go and surrender

responsibility. If I were to open a studio, that sacred time to surrender would be lost.

In addition to making time for the activities that fulfill us and
represent our core values, it's important to take the time to truly
connect with and evaluate *how* we make money. Those who are
resourceful and creatively find income streams that align with
their core values are not only much more successful but much
happier as well.

Ideally, we want to avoid the trap of doing something for money
that's not aligned with what we want out of life. We'll discuss
finding these income streams more specifically next week, but for
now I'd just like you to contrast your core values with how you are
earning money today. Does your current lifestyle contradict what
you value the most? Are you almost there? What changes could
you make today to be better aligned with your inner self?

WHY DO YOU WAKE UP IN THE MORNING?

Seriously. What motivates you to get out of bed every day? Is it to
make money? Is it to help others? Is it to support your family? Is
it to create? Or is it because it's what everyone else is doing?

If we want to live consciously and connected, we need to know
the answer to these important questions. When we don't have clarity
about what we want to do with the time we have, we end up in the
passenger seat. We might have nice success and a nice house and a
nice family and a nice income, but we never feel completely, authentically ourselves because we're living without a true purpose.

We need to know why we get out of bed in the morning. I've
developed a big, juicy exercise to help you further your discovery
of who you are as an individual. This exercise will help you define
what you truly want to create and why you want to create it. It will
help you answer all these tough questions.

Take a deep breath and prepare to feel uncomfortable. The
questions I'm about to ask—and that you're about to answer—can

seem overwhelming at first, especially if you haven't thought about them before. If you read some of the questions and have no clue how to respond, that is totally okay! The goal is to start expanding our hearts and our minds, to open them to greater possibility for the time we have on earth. Remember, our life is not a rehearsal—it's our one and only performance.

If money didn't matter, what would you do with your time?

What inspires you to wake up each day?

What activities make your heart sing?

Describe your perfect day. What activities are you doing?

Why do you want to create abundance?

What will you give to the world in return for the abundance you create?

What would you love your life to look like one year from today?

What do you believe are your greatest gifts?

Do you spend most of your time doing activities you love?

When do you feel most alive?

If you knew you could not fail, what would you do?

What do you believe is your greater purpose in life?

What drives you to dream big and live big?

Whom do you love most in the world?

What do you love doing most in the world?

How do you most love to contribute to the world?

What is your reason for being here on earth?

I know that these are truly big questions. Start your answers by creating bullet points for all the things that you would do if you didn't have to work or worry about money. What would you do with your free time? When you're stuck at work or having a busy week, what activities do you miss? When do you feel most child-like? When you experience flow or a rush of happiness, what are you doing?

Once you have your list, try to narrow down the points in a way that allows you to shape a sentence, a paragraph, or even a page. Write about what makes you feel alive, happy, and full of energy. Write about your passions, what you love, and when you feel in your greatest flow. We will call this your "why." There are full books and courses devoted to developing and creating your why. But for our purposes, we want to focus on creating intention, clarity, and a starting point for greatness.

With time, the why statement you create will grow, expand, and become more focused and clear. The point is to simply start somewhere. A why I started with was to be my most rested, healthy, and kind self. This is still true for me. With time, maturity, and contemplation, I have expanded and evolved my why. You are of course free to revise, expand, and revisit your why whenever you desire, but having a starting point is the key. Start somewhere and start today. Here is my why:

1. To elevate the state of consciousness and aligned living throughout the world

2. To practice and teach spiritual leadership around the world

3. To inspire others to take the lead for their health, their finances, their results, and their lives

Your why may not be anything like mine—and that's totally okay! Yours might be a paragraph or a full page. Mine started out that way, but with time, I found it felt right to shape my why into a three-piece clarity statement. It works for me.

For the purpose of Beautiful Money, there are only two guidelines for creating your why. First, it should make you smile and give you butterflies. Second, it should act as a guide and an intention behind what you will do with the abundance that's on its way. As such, your why should not only focus on yourself but should demonstrate how you plan to pay the results of this program forward and be a sparkplug for other people to dream bigger. The end goal is to create a clear statement that describes your reason for desiring Beautiful Money and how you intend to make the world a better place because of it.

Our why statement creates clarity and helps us move from a state of fear to a state of love and action. It helps us become more courageous, to make the big leaps and step away from conformity. Writing this statement on paper creates a significant and powerful intention in the world. The act of writing it down is affirming universally that you are asking for Beautiful Money and what you intend to give in return. Many people undervalue the powerful act of writing a why statement on paper. The commitment on paper creates a force and momentum that is difficult to describe and explain. You must take my word for it. As the saying goes, you have to believe it to see it.

Writing your why statement on paper also creates a loving sense of urgency in your life and acts as a reminder that your time on this earth is precious and temporary. Every day should be lived fully and on purpose.

This program is full of tricks and tips and exercises that will help you build a deep desire to stay on the path to Beautiful Money with fabulous momentum. The why statement is just one of these exercises. For most people, getting positive momentum started is the biggest challenge. This is why we start with our why.

A why statement that's deeply aligned with our innermost selves and our core values pulls us in the direction we want to go.

Writing it down shouts out vibrantly to the universe around you, "Yes! I am ready and committed to starting my abundant, joyful, and aligned journey *right now!*"

This is not to say that we don't all need some form of outside encouragement from time to time, because we do. But the goal of the why statement is to help build our inner resources so we need less help, validation, and momentum from others to reach our goals. It's just another piece of the Beautiful Money puzzle that helps us stop doing the shit we hate and step into the driver's seat in our lives. Your why will help you be more self-motivated, clearer, and more powerful within your day. It will remind you that there is no time to wake up frustrated and unhappy—there is only room for inspiration, creativity, and life-force energy.

You might be thinking, "Whoa Leanne! This is a huge assignment. I'm not sure what to say, or if I'm even ready to face the reasons why I'm reading this book." I assure you, I understand. Most of my clients experience a moment of complete brain freeze when contemplating their why statement for the first time. Believe me—I was there too!

I'd like to share an example from Beth, a student who took my Beautiful Money course in the spring of 2015.

She started with her list of core values, her four pillars:

Family

Community

Health

Spirituality

And then she answered my questions with a few bullet points:

If money didn't matter, what would you do with your time?

- I would volunteer
- I would work part time because I love the fact that my job helps other people
- I would travel
- I would spend as much time as I could with my husband, dogs, and relatives
- I would spend more time in nature and being active

What inspires you to wake up each day?

- Being able to spend time with my husband and dogs
- Helping people at work
- Connecting with myself and my higher power through living mindfully and being active in nature
- Just experiencing what life has to offer

Why do you want to create abundance?

- To be happier
- To feel less stressed, worried, and anxious about money
- To trust myself again
- To contribute to my family and community more

What do you believe is your greater purpose in life?

- To be a good friend, wife, and community member
- To serve others as much as, if not more than, I serve myself
- To live by example and aligned with my spiritual beliefs

What drives you to dream big and live big?

- The vastness of the world
- How positive I feel when I accomplish a goal or do something out of the ordinary that I wasn't sure I could do

What is your reason for being here on earth?

- Oh my God, I have no idea
- To help and inspire people to be more kind and patient

While you're drafting your why statement, it's totally okay to admit that you are unsure. Beth isn't alone in freaking out about not knowing why we're here on earth. It's a gigantic question. Not knowing what you want to answer is totally reasonable. I'd be more worried if you didn't take a moment to pause.

The goal is to contemplate *an* answer. You're not going to be graded. No answers are right or wrong, and I'm afraid there aren't any multiple-choice questions. Take a deep breath, trust your gut, and rely on your intuition to guide you.

Here is Beth's why statement, which she's admitted to revising a few times along the way:

I'm here to make the most of the opportunity to live as a human being. In order to do that, I need to take care of my body inside and out (with healthy food, exercise, and meditation) while also sharing my talents and skills with others to make the unique contribution to the world that only I can make.

I'm inspired to get up in the morning so I can spend time nurturing my family, my pets, and my community. I am inspired by nature and feel grateful to live surrounded by abundant beauty. I am most happy when I feel connected to my husband, my friends, my family, the earth, and the greater community.

I am driven to live big because I don't want to miss a moment of this gorgeous, delicious opportunity called our lives. If money didn't matter, I would live my life in a way that is similar to the way I do now, but I would like to travel more and constantly be looking for new experiences to expand my world and challenge myself. My core values to creating Beautiful Money are family, community, health, and spirituality.

YOUR BEAUTIFUL MONEY VISION BOARD

Our why statement is just one tool that helps pull us toward creating abundance and holistic wealth. I also ask all my students and clients to create a vision board (which is sometimes called a "dream board" or even a "vision map"). This might seem a little cheesy at first, but it can be immensely powerful in helping us move forward and change our lives. With all my heart and soul, I assure you that avoiding making a vision board will only delay abundance, joy, alignment, and clarity. Creating one as soon as possible will put you on the absolute fast track to creating Beautiful Money. Here's why.

Our minds think in pictures, so having a visual representation of our why statement that we see every day is an essential tool for creating Beautiful Money. Find a series of photos, quotes, or other visual representations of your why statement. You can include magazine clippings, photos (of yourself, your family, inspirational people, even celebrities), short quotes, affirmations, or simply pictures of what you want your life to look like over the next six months to a year. These photos, words, and statements should raise your energy and uplift your soul every time you look at them.

A vision board should keep us motivated and moving toward our goals on a daily basis. As such, every single thing you add to your vision board should be aligned with your core values and what you want to create. There should be a sense of anticipation, of excitement, of a desire deep down inside your gut that *this* is what you want.

We all know people who make vision boards but don't end up with any results. Here's why: The magic happens when the mind is able to draw a picture of our destination *and* connect with us emotionally to stir up the feelings required to take action. The secret here is that your mind alone cannot turn a vision board into reality. The pictures on the board must deeply connect with your heart and soul. Only then will your emotional state churn up those fabulous feelings of inspiration, excitement, and joy. The feelings are the magic ingredient to give you the motivation to take action.

Beautiful Money Tip

A LOT OF EXPERTS suggest making vision boards for the next five or even ten years. But for me, that makes my goals feel *too* far away. I find that for most people, a shorter time period helps to create a loving sense of urgency that allows them to truly connect with their goals.

I like to create annual vision boards because a year is just enough time to keep me motivated and emotionally invested, but whatever feels comfortable to you is fine.

If you make your vision board only from your head and what you think you want, not much will change. Emotional alignment is the secret to making what's on a vision board come to fruition. If we're not emotionally invested, if we feel uncertain about our ability to make our dreams reality, or if we have designed our vision board to look like someone else's, we are going to get stagnant results. If we have no skin in the game, we will never feel motivated to take action. We can hire all the coaches in the world and take all the courses available, but external motivation will never be powerful enough to turn our vision board into reality. That motivation must come from within. Self-motivated people get shit done and are the most resourceful people on the planet. We may need the occasional pep talk when we get knocked down, but we bounce back up and move onward. Self-motivated people are emotionally intelligent and spend little time on drama and trivial matters.

You may feel you're too busy right now to make a vision board. Maybe you'll put it off till next month, and next month. . . . This will become your number one regret. Right now, creating a vision board is the priority. It is a priority above checking e-mails, running errands, booking meetings, cleaning your house, and anything else that is on your to-do list. Make space and time to create your vision board now. I am speaking from my heart when I say that it is absolutely necessary for creating Beautiful Money. Most people who lack Beautiful Money in their lives also lack a fully connected, vibrant, and clear vision board. If you do currently have a board, take a good look at it. If it doesn't stir up hyperexcited and wild passion, your vision board is likely lacking life force. Start fresh and create one that sets your soul on fire.

Beautiful Money Tip

POPULAR WAY TO display your vision board is to frame it and mount it somewhere in your home where you will see it often, but I've had clients who simply post pictures above their desk at work or even on the bathroom mirror. Just make sure you see your vision board often every day. Finding a beautiful and luxurious frame for it is a fabulous way to show how valuable its meaning is to you!

When you're finished with the first iteration of your vision board, take a break. Walk away. After a few hours, revisit it. Does it fire you up emotionally? Can you feel positive energy deep in your body? If not, concentrate on this question: What do you want to do, be, and have? After a few moments of reflection, write down your answers. These should be your deepest desires and dreams. Use visual representations of what you've written down to create a vision board. (This is also a good trick if you revisit your first board and realize that it's basically great but one or two pieces are not quite right.)

Admittedly, even the absolute best Beautiful Money vision board isn't a magic wand. There's always going to come a day when we feel unmotivated, uninspired, or just lazy. It's impossible to be "on" all the time. We're going to have off days. However, your vision board should inspire, encourage, and energize you to be a little bit better every day.

Your vision board is a loving reminder to keep plugging away even if you don't feel like it and even when you feel the world is against you. It is your source of life-force energy when you feel you don't have any. We still need mentors, friends, and loved ones to support us, but this week is all about building momentum from the inside out.

STEP TWO:
CONQUER FEAR WITH COURAGE

Figuring out what your core values are and crafting a why statement are just the first steps in adopting a Beautiful Money mindset. We also need to examine what is happening with our mental and emotional state so we can learn how to align what we think and feel with what we do. Bringing how we think and feel into action always results in holistic wealth and abundance. It is the only way to churn up the self-motivation necessary to take confident steps toward what you truly desire.

HOLISTIC THINKING

We often let our minds overshadow our hearts. But Beautiful Money requires a more holistic approach in which we understand that our mental state and our emotions are inexorably linked.

Simply put, our hearts are the true powerhouses for abundance and greatness. But to live our lives emotionally well, we must learn how to take charge of our thoughts. Our hearts may not need any training, but our minds do.

Our hearts have no desire or use for drama, but, left untrained, our minds can't get enough. That's because the mind is wired for survival. Its job is to spot potential problems and focus on nothing else until that problem is resolved. This is helpful when a threat is real and pressing, but often the mind creates drama and stress out of thin air. Over time, this becomes a trap of negative emotions and can create a downward spiral in which we fixate on what's going wrong or, worse, what could go wrong. On the flip side, we exist in a healthy and happy emotional state when we are thinking positive, empowering, and inspired thoughts.

So although we must lead with our heart to create Beautiful Money, we also need to develop amazing mental muscle power to maintain careful control over our mind and the thoughts that pass through it.

Beautiful Money requires us to be strategic and action oriented, to be sure, but, even more important, we need to train our brain to work in alignment with our desired outcome. In the upcoming pages, I'm going to offer you some tools and strategies to help you do just that.

To learn how we can create a positive emotional state with our thoughts, we must have a basic conversation about the subconscious mind. Our subconscious mind is our data storage tank. We program what we put into this storage tank with our conscious, "thinking" mind. It's important to understand that the subconscious mind cannot reason or judge—those are tasks our conscious mind controls. The function of our subconscious mind is essentially to store whatever data we give it. All our experiences are stored and remembered in our subconscious mind. But although the subconscious basically acts as a mental and emotional storage unit, we have the ability to control the way it handles what we put in there. Experts who study the brain—including psychologists, psychiatrists, and neurologists—have varying opinions about exactly what our subconscious mind does, but they tend to agree that it both controls our emotions and is capable of learning. Dr. Matthew B. James, writing for *Psychology Today*, explains that in order to protect us, "The unconscious stays alert and tries to glean . . . lessons from each experience."[7] This, in turn, affects our emotions. If we've had prior success in a particular area—say, sports or academic achievement—we are more likely to feel positive and energized when an athletic or academic task comes up.

However, our subconscious mind is limited in its ability to interpret. Its capabilities are extremely basic. It needs clear directions. Like a dog or a child, the subconscious mind takes instructions literally. And many of the "beliefs" it follows no longer serve us cognitively. Again, our subconscious mind cannot judge or reason. It just runs whatever program we give it. When it comes to money and creating abundance, those subconscious, ingrained beliefs can work against us. The emotional data stored in our subconscious mind often reflects negative thoughts and experiences. Our data storage tank is filled with negative beliefs and ideas about ourself and how we handle money. If our subconscious mind is programmed to trigger thoughts of scarcity, fear, lack, and frustration around money, it will be impossible to create Beautiful Money.

That's why we begin by learning how to retrain our subconscious mind. Luckily, it is a great student and is incredibly coachable. We can actually change how we think and feel (our overall mind-set, from a psychological perspective) by revising the kind of associations that are triggered in our minds at the subconscious level. If we want to change the way we think about money and ourselves consciously, we need to change our behavior at a conscious level *and* retrain our brains at the subconscious level.

Confused? Let's try this again. We must retrain our subconscious by first consciously deciding to accept only Beautiful Money thoughts and by tossing out negative, victim, or scarcity thoughts. We must be in the driver's seat in our thinking. If we don't take conscious charge of our thoughts, we are basically letting our subconscious backseat driver take charge. We have taken our hands off the wheel, allowing whatever has been stored in our subconscious to inform what we do and believe about ourselves.

However, once we are aware that we can change and control our relationship with our subconscious mind, we can mentally fake it until we make it. We can use a variety of tools and techniques to do this. At first, these tools are necessary because we may not always believe the thoughts that we actually desire. (If we did, we wouldn't need to change our subconscious mind.) Think about it this way: We may want to be prosperous and radiantly healthy, but today we're broke and overweight. But believing this can happen is a huge step.

To reprogram our subconscious mind, we need to dig up every inch of leadership and confidence that we can find in our bodies and have the courage to trust that our desired state—of holistic abundance and wealth—is already on its way. This is not an easy task in the beginning. I still get tripped up by it every once in a while and have to remind myself that tools are there to help me.

We can use the fact that the subconscious mind has little room for interpretation to our advantage. We can retrain our subconscious by changing the way we think and using repetition to train and revise what is stored in that part of our brain. It takes practice, but as we train our minds to work more harmoniously with our desired results and feelings, we begin to live more peacefully, harmoniously, and abundantly.

Week Two is focused on changing the way we think and behave so we will be in alignment with Beautiful Money. In this particular step, I share the practical tools that will help you change the way you think and behave forever. Let's get started.

LOVE AND MONEY

Emotions are truly the source of Beautiful Money. In our busy daily lives, we might think our minds are the powerhouse of our lives and experiences, but actually the powerhouse is our hearts. A study published in 2004 concluded that the heart's electrical field is about a hundred times stronger than that of the brain, and the heart's magnetic field is about five thousand times stronger than the brain's.[8] This is why our hearts are so important for creating Beautiful Money.

But our emotions don't just happen to us. Feelings just happen, but emotion requires thought. How we feel is based on the energy generated from our hearts. Our feelings become emotions when our thoughts mix with and interpret our feelings.

We must recognize that our feelings and emotions are different. Feelings originate from our heart, but our overall emotional state at any given moment is the result of our minds mixing with and interpreting these feelings. This is evidence of the basic mind-body connection that exists for everyone, in numerous ways. That's why the same situation can make us feel happier or sadder depending on what else is going on in our environment. The feeling itself doesn't change, but our thoughts and our interpretation of that feeling can. This is one reason why it's important to be in the driver's seat when it comes to our thoughts: they drive our emotions. We simply cannot take advantage of all the positive feelings we experience if our thoughts aren't positive and aligned.

When we live in the passenger seat and let our thoughts run wild, our emotions can quickly spiral into a hot mess of debt, drama, chaos, and a roller coaster of emotions. When people feel "moody," it's a good indication that their thoughts are running amok. That's why we practice detachment and use tools to reframe our thoughts so that what we think and feel will help us along the path to Beautiful Money instead of throwing up roadblocks all the time.

What most of us don't realize is that the key role of our brain is to keep us alive. We have to remember that although we live in a crazy-paced technologically altered world that makes all kinds of demands on our brain, our brain's core function is to keep us safe and out of danger. Positive thinking is like the mental version of getting into shape: it requires commitment, discipline, and repetition.

Our ultimate goal is to avoid attaching feelings to thoughts that aren't aligned with where we want to be, so we no longer feel shitty and hard on ourselves. We can choose to take control and think our way to wealth. But most people don't have that level of awareness. Most people unconsciously attach feelings to every thought that comes into their mind. (Or, if not every thought, a vast majority of them.)

Once we are aware of the link between our thoughts and our emotions, as well as that between the conscious and subconscious minds, we can start filtering information. By practicing disciplined thinking and using other tools, we can actually rewire our subconscious mind to value the positive aspects of life and rid ourselves of beliefs about ourselves and the world that are no longer serving us. And when we get really great at tossing out negative, misaligned thoughts while embracing positive and aligned thoughts, we are able to play a more active role in how we live.

AWARENESS IS POWER

BEAUTIFUL MONEY REQUIRES us to be mindful and aware of how our thoughts directly influence our feelings, which in turn affects our actions. Awareness is really the starting point. Once we are aware of how our mind works, we can practice filtering one thought at a time. We will learn to become keenly aware and very protective of what thoughts we choose to accept.

With practice, we learn to detach from thoughts that don't serve us well. We let negative and destructive thoughts pass, without attachment, like clouds in the sky.

I like to picture my thoughts as cars passing along a road. When a car containing negative, snarky, mean, or judgmental thoughts approaches, I let that car go on its way. However, when a passing car is full of energy, light, and creativity, I visualize that car pulling over. Then I purposefully attach positive feelings to it, and wish it well on its journey. This might sound a bit silly, but I know that by being conscious of my thoughts, I choose the vehicles that create my feelings and shape my overall mood each and every day.

The easiest way for us to begin disciplining our thinking is to observe our thoughts. Practice letting negativity pass by and purposely paying more attention to positive and uplifting thoughts. From there, you can dive in even deeper and ask yourself, Does this thought I'm having align with my core values and the reason why I'm creating Beautiful Money?

Keep in mind that, like yoga and meditation, disciplined thinking is a practice. Most of us have allowed our unconscious mind total control over our feelings for years, if not decades. It takes time to rewire the patterns that we've created. You'll have days when the control you have over your thoughts is awesome and powerful and successful, and days when you feel overwhelmed by negativity no matter what you do. That's okay and to be expected. Simply know that your effort alone is what matters.

By practicing disciplined thinking, we not only help elevate our mood and outlook overall but also teach ourselves how our thoughts directly affect our feelings. Disciplined thinking is an important skill that requires lifelong daily practice. You won't ever master it, but I promise that you will get better at it.

AFFIRM ABUNDANCE

As we're starting our journey, I really believe in using affirmations to help us get into the state in which momentum, magic, and change truly happen. A repetitive affirmation practice can rewire our subconscious and help us replace the negative beliefs we've gathered about ourselves with positive, empowering ones.

According to Merriam-Webster, to affirm is "to say that something is true in a confident way," or "to show a strong belief in or dedication to (something, such as an important idea)."[9] By any definition, the role of affirmations is to provide support and encouragement. These simple sayings are an important tool that helps us to believe in ourselves and minimize the negativity, threats, and uncertainty of the outside world. And when used over time, affirmations change our thoughts, emotions, and behavior. By using affirmations, we can rewire our brain and react differently to the world around us.

Even the scientific world is taking a look at affirmations. A recent meta-analysis (in which researchers examine multiple studies looking for similar findings) published in *Health Psychology* demonstrated that using affirmations helped people to change unhealthy habits like smoking and overeating just as much as, if not more than, conventional interventions.[10] The researchers noted that when used habitually over time, affirmations change the way our brain responds to the types of thinking that could be constituted as a threat. This makes sense, given what we now know about the unconscious mind and how it controls our thoughts, which then affects our feelings and behaviors.

Beautiful Money Tip

YOUR VISION BOARD is one of the most powerful tools to help you focus your thinking. Your subconscious mind is working 24-7, so the more you focus your eyes and attention on your vision board, the more abundantly and peacefully you will sleep at night. This is a loving reminder to make sure you have completed your vision board already!

The science proves that we actually can fake it until we make it. When we first start saying an affirmation like "Beautiful Money is on its way every day," we may feel a little hokey. I know I did. But over time, we begin to believe in whatever message we are telling ourselves over and over again. Eventually, we feel that statement at a deeper level and no longer need to say it out loud. The end result is internalizing our affirmations and supporting ourselves from a place deep within, which creates the confidence and momentum needed to change our behavior and attract holistic wealth.

But that's not all. A study published by the Public Library of Science supported previous evidence that affirmations can protect us from the effects of stress and demonstrated how continuing to use affirmations over time can improve our ability to solve problems and may even improve academic achievement.[11] As more and more scientists research the connection between the unconscious mind, affirmations, and real-life behavioral changes, I suspect the perception of these important tools will change. But in the meantime, we can harness the power of affirmations for ourselves.

At their core, affirmations are tools that allow us to shift our emotional state so we can be focused in a more abundant (and less fearful) direction. My favorite affirmation, which I include at the beginning of every course I teach (and have framed in my home), is:

Today beauty, abundance, and grace are flowing my way.

This is an affirmation I love to use on a daily basis. It helps me start and finish my day in a place of abundance. Another fabulous affirmation tip I love comes from *The Power of Your Subconscious Mind*, by Dr. Joseph Murphy. He suggests repeating the word "wealth" to yourself slowly and quietly for about five minutes prior to sleep. He explains that this practice helps your subconscious mind to prioritize wealth in your conscious experiences.[12] I love this idea!

Beautiful Money
AFFIRMATIONS

HERE ARE MORE of my favorite affirmations from the Beautiful Money course:

- Every day, in every way, Beautiful Money is on its way.
- Today Beautiful Money is flowing my way.
- Today is a Beautiful Money day.
- I always align how I spend my time with what is most precious and important to me.
- I have more than enough time to get everything done. I am in no rush.
- I fall asleep tonight with a deep feeling of gratitude for all I have and all that is on its way.
- Each and every night, I sleep wealthy.
- I nurture my body, mind, and soul with excellence.
- I am in the most abundant and healthy state of my life.
- I am mindful that I will see it when I believe it.
- I am healthy, wealthy, and free.
- Both awake and asleep, I am a magnet for money.
- My creativity is the key to Beautiful Money.
- I make more money than ever before, doing what I love.
- I soar to my success by helping everyone around me soar to their success.
- I am worthy of wealth.
- Life force is my money magnet.
- I commit to excellence every day.
- Love and kindness are my money magnets.
- I always leave myself open to new possibilities, elevated thinking, and higher levels of abundance.
- I am ready for great wealth.

- I get wealthier and wealthier every day.
- The more I nurture and take care of myself, the more money I make.
- I am worthy of Beautiful Money. I deserve the very best life has to offer.
- I am a master money manager.
- I am worth it.
- My natural state is beautiful abundance.
- Creating wealth is a simple process.
- I am divinely debt-free.
- In every cell of my body, I know that my natural state is one of abundance and love and well-being.
- My body knows exactly what to do. I tune in to my intuition and know that I am greatness. I already have all the answers. I am abundant.
- I say yes to aligning with beautiful, abundant, joyful, and holistic wealth.
- I choose love over fear.
- I make subtle shifts today that will result in greatness tomorrow.
- I love myself more today. I love my life more today.
- I consciously design my life today.
- I am patient, kind, and powerful.
- I am a visionary. I always start with the end in mind.
- I rid my life of chaos and make space daily for Beautiful Money.
- I am crystal clear on the few activities in my life that create Beautiful Money.
- I focus all my attention and energy on what I truly desire.
- My creativity, compassion, and clarity will bring me great wealth.

VISUALIZE IT

Our minds think in pictures, so get busy filling yours with fabulous ones! Visualization is also a fabulous practice to commit to, and your vision board is an important tool to utilize while trying to craft more positive thoughts. Anytime you have a moment, close your eyes and let your beautiful mind wander around your ideal, dream world.

For a deeper visualization practice, sit on the floor in a quiet, dark room. (I prefer to do this when I have twenty or thirty minutes completely to myself, without distractions.) Get comfortable and put on inspirational music. Close your eyes and picture the exact outcome you desire. I like to visualize this as my own mental movie. This requires a relaxed state and mind-body connection. You cannot rush your Beautiful Money mind movie. If you have overpacked your day and overloaded your to-do list, you might have difficulty seeing anything when you sit down. I encourage you to get in the habit of scheduling time (at least in the beginning) to do this practice. The more you do this, the more momentum you will create toward making what you visualize, either in your practice or on your vision board, reality.

The more space we have in our life, our body, and our mind, the more powerful and effective our visualization practice will be. That's just another reason to regularly cleanse physical, emotional, and mental clutter!

GET IN THE MOOD (TO MEDITATE)

I have to confess that I am not yet a consistent meditator. But I desire to be! Still, I rarely feel in the mood to meditate. That's because my default behavior is to be busy. But we're not often in the mood to do the things that need to be done. When was the last time you were in the mood to sort your receipts, do your tax return, or clean out your juicer? There might be the odd being who loves these activities, but most of us don't.

Meditation is the simplest and most perfect exercise to boost our awareness that our brain loves to be busy just to be busy. If you stop and just let your mind flow, like you do in a meditative state, you'll see a million thoughts zipping around like race cars on a track. But practicing meditation helps us practice simplicity, slowing those cars until they exit and the entire track is empty. Achieving a simplistic, quiet mind can help us to be more present more often and to build the consciousness needed to practice disciplined thinking. Meditation is a perfect tool for becoming a practitioner of thought detachment. But it can be hard for people to incorporate into their daily lives.

Beautiful Money Tip

*I*F YOU ARE new to meditation, check out the App Store for your smartphone or computer! There are numerous free meditation apps (Calm is my favorite) that offer guided meditation and affirmations to help you on your Beautiful Money journey.

If you're like me, meditation might not be difficult—sitting still isn't hard for me—but you may never feel superpsyched to practice it on a regular basis. In the past, I have gone on meditation retreats, practiced guided meditation, and occasionally made the time to meditate for a few days in a row.

But recently I decided to surrender to the fact that, in the moment, a walking meditation works better for me. Walking meditation was my perfect starting place. And I'm still there. I am a sensitive soul and need time alone to process, contemplate, and create. When I don't have that time-out, I sign up for every course, commit to launching ten programs in a month, become a workaholic, and eventually lose my patience for everything and everyone.

WALKING MEDITATION

FOR THE PURPOSE of Beautiful Money, walking meditation is a simple practice. Put on a pair of comfortable shoes (sneakers, gym shoes, even ballet flats are great) and some comfy clothes, and go! Sometimes I bring my iPod and put on some calming music, but I often choose silence. If you feel like listening to music, that's great too! My only "rule" during my walking meditation is no talking. Others might have a more structured walking meditation practice, but my practice works for me.

The practice is about letting go. I find walking near water is very healing, and I often choose to walk along the lake near my home. Your only work is to be silent, move your body, and detach from your mind. You will find your mind wants to think about what you should be doing or how unproductive this meditation walk is. You might start thinking about work or something that has emotionally triggered you recently. All kinds of busy thoughts are going to pop into your head! When thoughts pop up (especially ones that generate an emotional response), take a deep breath and come back to the present.

The objective of this walk is to practice connection with yourself and the world around you. Walking meditation is especially helpful for souls, like me, who can easily become distracted, unnecessarily busy, or ungrounded.

If you live near trails or water, your walking meditations will be very healing! Every time your mind starts to fire up, practice tossing the thoughts into the air around you. Looking at nature as you walk by, especially trees that have been in place for decades, is very helpful in regaining connection.

What is most fascinating to me is how peaceful nature is. Everything is working so divinely; the whole ecosystem seems effortless and right. Walking meditation always brings me back to being connected to myself and to the earth below my feet. Practicing mental silence during a walking meditation is not always easy, but with practice it gets easier. The better you get, the more healing your walks will be and the more connected you will feel to your highest self and the world around you. Walking meditation is also a great tool to help you loosen up and expel any unwanted energy stored in your body.

The good news is that I have developed a keen awareness for when I start to become a spaz. I have become pretty good at recognizing the symptoms of when I am starting to creep up on this state of mind, and that's when I know that I need to go on a walking meditation and fit in a yoga class. I got really great at being present—and then I had kids and got bumped back to meditation kindergarten. I'm relearning how to be present and connected as a mom. My husband and I even built a meditation balcony outside our bedroom. I figured that having a physical place to meditate could help me advance my practice to seated meditation. Don't get me wrong: I love my walking meditation, but somewhere deep down in my soul I now crave a more formal meditation practice. I always trust that I am exactly where I am supposed to be. For years, a consistent seated meditation practice wasn't a priority. I guess I wasn't ready. It took me until the age of forty to feel ready and excited for a more formal, seated meditation practice. I guess what I mean to say is, don't be hard on yourself if you feel disconnected or a little lost but not fully ready for or committed to daily meditation. What is important is that you have an image of where you would like to be, what state or place you yearn to end up in.

Whether you love meditation or not (and whether you practice it right now or not), we all need help using the tools the universe presents us. For me, walking meditation is a way of slowing down my mind that gives me time and space to detach from my negative or disempowering thoughts. Regardless of how absent or advanced your meditation practice is, it is the perfect tool for training yourself to detach from your thinking. There is no perfect way to meditate. The goal of meditation is stillness and connection. Drop your book right now, close your eyes, and do your best not to think for one minute. If you can do it without much of a problem, you are likely already an advanced practitioner.

MORE THOUGHTFUL TOOLS

Affirmations, meditation, and visualization aren't the only ways to change how we think about and see the world around us. Another way is to find fabulous mentors—whether actual people you create a relationship with or simply courses, audio programs, videos, podcasts, and workshops. Tools are your BFFs for building up mental muscles.

I must admit that I am a love and leadership junkie. I love reading books on personal development, spirituality, psychology, money management, leadership, business strategy, and more. I love TED Talks and podcasts in which experts and researchers share their insights. I love courses and groups that I can participate in and that teach me something new and improve my life and the lives of the people close to me. I love making relationships that are mutually beneficial both personally and professionally.

Learning inspires me to lead more and to wake up each day with purpose. Doing activities that help me grow as a person aligns both with my core values and with the reason why I want to attract, practice, and teach Beautiful Money. That said, your mentorship tools might be different. You may find podcasts boring but love reading books. Any activity or relationship that helps you feel aligned with your core values and in an elevated state of energy can be a tool to help mentor you on your journey to holistic abundance. I often listen to audiobooks or podcasts when I run— it's a fabulous way to combine two activities I love.

MY SELF-CONFIDENCE CHEAT SHEET

WHILE I WAS writing this book, I had a delicious conversation with one of my dear friends and mentors, Melanie Smith. It truly inspired me (you must check out her website: www.melaniesmithwll.com). We talked about how necessary traits like courage, confidence, self-esteem, and self-worth are for success. I have to admit that when talking to mentors, one of my favorite topics is how to fill up our self-love and courage tank!

That's because, on a personal level, I am not always superconfident. In my work, I see people who are like me— committed but not always confident—every day. I think it's important that we work on building our self-confidence and feelings of self-worth no matter where we are at.

What I lack in confidence, I make up in courage. That's a trait I have that others may not. One reason I am able to take big leaps despite my shaky confidence is that I am not afraid to fail. I don't get excited about failing, but I'm not afraid of it. Over the past two years, I've had my share of so-called failures, but I'm still standing strong! Despite my "shortcomings" I've also had two more babies, written a book (that I love), learned a ridiculous amount about the publishing industry, launched my blog and podcast, and spoken internationally.

On the outside, I probably seem superconfident, but this isn't always true. I question myself, I have moments when I feel like giving up, and I occasionally bawl my eyes out! The trick is to learn how to get my feet back on the ground, to learn how to get back in my groove, and to always, always, always persist!

First, acknowledge the traits you already have that help you be confident and make moves to create Beautiful Money. When you've done that, here are a few of my favorite tricks and tips to help build up your kick-ass self:

1. Strengthen your core

   A strong core helps us feel tall, powerful, and in control. You don't need a six-pack, but doing some planks, crunches, and abdominal exercises will make you feel like a badass and help your posture.

2. Talk to yourself!

   Affirmations like "I am strong, confident, and superhot" will absolutely help you get in a great groove. We've talked about the power of affirmations already, but remember that the moments before you fall asleep are the perfect time to program your subconscious mind.

When you put yourself to bed and wake up in the morning, affirm your very own power statement out loud. There is no time like today to start programming your subconscious to work in the direction of your dreams.

3. Do something scary

Building self-confidence requires you to do things you wouldn't normally do. The right amount of fear is when you are almost really, really afraid, but you don't feel like totally barfing. A great example is my client Becca. She was always afraid of jumping into water, but her husband surprised her with an experience in Hawaii in which she could ride a zip line safely into a shallow pond. Becca admitted to me that she was scared as hell when she grabbed the zip line, but with her husband's support and the cheers of everyone else at the zip line that day, she did it! And not only that, but by the end of the day Becca was jumping off the zip line— backward! That's how much she enjoyed overcoming her fear and seeing that the worry about jumping into water was (mostly) in her head.

Confidence is strengthened by experiences and through taking action. If you have a deep desire to be the most confident (and graceful) person you know, set a goal to complete a task that scares you but doesn't make you want to vomit or run away. A good way to get started overcoming your fears is to set a goal that deep in your gut you know you could achieve but that will require your full attention, commitment, and your greatest self showing up to go through with it—just like Becca did.

4. Find a confidant

There is nothing more healing than getting feelings of vulnerability or fear out of your body by verbally expressing how you feel. If you don't have someone in your life whom you completely trust and can be open with, journaling can be a great tool too.

5. Surround yourself with fabulous people

I can't emphasize this enough: When you have amazing people around you, you cannot help but soar! I love surrounding myself with people who lift me up and challenge me to be at my best.

Find a few people to surround yourself with who are doing the things you want to do but are scared to do. These don't have to be mentors per se but can just be friends and peers you admire. When I am around someone who is already living in my desired state, I get a glimpse of my own future, which is supercool. If your social circle isn't inspiring you or, worse yet, is dragging you down, perhaps it is time to find new friends!

6. Move your body

It doesn't have to be an intense workout, but physical movement has a way of making us feel better about ourselves. Try saying power statements like "I am powerful" or "I am life force" or "I am ready for greatness" in your head the next time you work out, do yoga, or go for a run.

7. **Don't be afraid to fail**

   Our greatest success often arrives after a failure or two (or three). The most powerful and visionary leaders typically experience the most failure. Embrace failure by looking at it differently. Failures are opportunities to learn from. Live boldly and shine brightly. When we fail, we're in the good company of others who would rather put their hearts and souls into something and fail than never try anything truly great.

8. **Commit to action**

   It's really tough building confidence while sitting on the bench. Being in a state of aligned action is how you will strengthen your self-confidence. However, it's important to be strategic because we need to move forward with attention and focus. When you hit a speed bump, take a moment or a day to have a little breakdown, but always get back up and try, try again.

Having extraordinary people as mentors is truly a powerful force. There is nothing more inspiring than sitting in a room with someone who is where you want to be. It's great if you can afford to mentor with someone wildly successful, but it's also easy to find mentors in your community.

Ask to interview a senior colleague at work, or simply ask someone you admire out for a coffee or a drink. A recent example from my life is that my husband, Ric, and I recently met a couple on our street and were invited over for a party. This couple lives in my dream house. Just being in their home gave me physical power for my visualization practice. I walked through it, felt the furniture, and observed every inch of the place.

Finding mentors doesn't have to happen within the confines of a formal program. Sometimes just a few moments chatting with someone who has achieved what you want to achieve can change your thoughts and your life. Without knowing it, the couple we met became Beautiful Money mentors for me and Ric. There's no need to overcomplicate mentorship. Often when you encounter someone who has the energy and health you desire, just being in his or her energy space will serve you more than words.

Beautiful Money Tip

IN ORDER TO find a mentor, you may have to look outside your social and professional circles. A great mentor is someone who has been where you are now but has moved past the challenges you are currently facing and landed where you desire to be.

Because I am an advocate of holistic wealth, I choose mentors who have created wealth in an aligned way. I feel inspired by people who take a holistic approach to wealth creation and who don't compromise their values on the path to making money. My favorite mentors are those who are in radiant health, are emotionally and financially free, and are authentically kind. These people are out there, and when you focus your attention on finding them, you will cross paths. When you do find them, turn off your ego and drink up every ounce of wisdom offered.

By using these tools and practices on a daily basis, we consciously start to shift our emotions. As we practice detachment and begin to let go of negative or self-defeating thoughts, we can change how our thinking interacts with how we feel. Over time, this practice can and will transform our lives completely.

A more conscious, resilient mind-set helps retrain the subconscious and rebuilds the foundation that we use to perceive the world around us. Instead of living from a place of fear or doubt, we become almost childlike and live in a state of curiosity, wonder, and excitement. Our newfound positivity helps us smile at the world and see that we are creative forces working in alignment with the entire natural world. And that, in turn, helps us believe that Beautiful Money is on its way.

STEP THREE:
ABUNDANCE IS AN INSIDE JOB

The Beautiful Money program is in part about practical shifts in money management, but, more important, it is also about the mental and emotional shifts required to create holistic wealth. One of the biggest changes we need to make is how we think about, well, nearly everything!

We have already started this work by making room for the great, both physically and emotionally, and by beginning to use tools to transform our mind-set. But the purpose of shifting our thoughts is to move from a place of fear, where we *hope* good things will happen, to a place of confidence, where we *expect* success and wealth. In order to truly create Beautiful Money, we need to know deep down that the lifestyle we desire *will* become a reality. We need to *know*, not just hope, that success and wealth are on the way.

You may be thinking, "Leanne, isn't hope a good thing?" And you're right. Hope as an abstract concept is good. Hope can be nice, hope can be positive, and hope for great results can provide us with the initial motivation we need to make a change in our lives. But when all we do is *hope* that we will achieve our goals and live in a way that's aligned with our core values, we do not have the proper fuel to create lasting change.

Beautiful Money Tip

*T*HERE'S A REASON I love yoga, walking meditation, posting affirmations in my home, and creating vision boards year after year. Everyone needs tools to support their growth and leadership development. Until you become an absolute master at turning your dreams into reality, lean on your favorite tools (including those described in step two) to help in your development. If you leave your life to chance, or to your current state of thinking, not much transformation will occur.

Like most people, my client Mel thought hoping for good things would be enough. She texted me: "Leanne, I am hoping that money and success is on its way." I immediately texted this message back: "Your homework is to shift to a place of absolute knowing. Instead of hoping that money and success are on their way, work on shifting your emotional state to a place of expecting that you will achieve all your goals and become financially free."

There was a pause, and then Mel replied, "How am I supposed to do that?"

In step two, I showed you how you can harness the power of your thinking to result in a positive emotional experience. We also talked about detaching from negative thoughts and using tools and practices to focus your attention on what you desire most.

The next step forward, which we will discuss here, is to use your mental power to shift your emotional state from one of *hop-*

ing to one of *expecting*. Expectation is the perfect fuel for turning your vision board into reality. Being hopeful just isn't powerful enough to create your desired outcome or to turn your dreams into reality. For the purposes of this book, consider hope as the watered-down version of expectation. Having faith and confidence in yourself and the universe is key to becoming a person who expects greatness.

So, what is the "real" difference between hoping and expecting? When we simply hope for things to happen, we put ourselves in a sort of metaphysical limbo. Like being "fine," hoping absolves us of the responsibility, power, and control we have over what happens in our lives. In that way, hope can actually be negative and play a role in holding us back.

In contrast, when we *expect* to reach our goals, to feel happy, to achieve whatever success we're aiming for, we live confidently, powerfully, and courageously. We have a sense of anticipation and excitement. We are eager to see what happens next. We know that whatever happens, the universe has our back. And knowing that, in turn, creates an unshakable sense of positivity and confidence and wonder in our lives. When we mix hoping with a healthy dose of confidence, faith, and courage, the outcome is expectation.

DO YOU EXPECT GOOD THINGS OR BAD THINGS?

SO MANY OF us have learned to expect the worst. When we're in that frame of mind, it's easy to concentrate on our fears of what *could* happen. It's as if we expect to fail in every scenario we encounter.

When we begin to think that way, we prime ourselves to minimize, or even completely eliminate, the likelihood of a positive outcome. Creating Beautiful Money requires us to think more creatively and intentionally. When we practice disciplined thinking, we learn to watch out for and observe automatic reactions. If we encounter a situation in which we instantly think that something bad is going to happen or assume that we will fail no matter what, we can and should take a step back. We can take a moment to get connected and evaluate the reality and the likelihood that the worst-case scenario will come to pass. Typically, it's not very likely at all!

That moment of awareness allows us to reframe the situation and break the cycle of automatically assuming the worst from the world around us—a symptom of acting from a place of fear. Instead, we can choose to revise what we tell ourselves about that particular scenario, practicing compassion and expecting the best from the world around us, which allows us to act from a place of abundance and positivity.

So how do we transition from a state of fear and hoping to a state of confidence and expectation? I like this quote from Benjamin Mee, author of the book (and movie) *We Bought a Zoo*: "You know, sometimes all you need is twenty seconds of insane courage, just literally twenty seconds of embarrassing bravery, and I promise you something great will come of it."[13] Rest assured, you don't have to buy a zoo in order to create Beautiful Money. But you do have to take a leap of faith that the universe (or whatever higher power you believe in) has your back.

EMBRACE THE DIVINE

I believe that the power of the divine is showering down on us all the time, and that we all have infinite access to life force and creative power. But what is the divine? I find that the flow of power often appears in the form of a brilliant idea that arrives seemingly out of nowhere, an inspiring (sometimes lucid) dream, or a flash of creative expression like song lyrics, writing, music, or art.

To me, faith in the divine doesn't have to be religious, though it can be. Having faith in something bigger than yourself is the master ingredient for developing trust that the universe has your back.

Although inspiration can strike us at any time, it flows in most powerfully when we're in a relaxed state. For me, it happens when I'm doing yoga, listening to music, or going for a walk or run. As a musician, Ric often finds this state at night, or right before he goes to sleep. Sometimes he'll wake up in the middle of the night with an idea for a song. My friend Meg feels divine inspiration while running or enjoying a walk with her dogs.

We are most likely to receive inspiration and to acknowledge it as something to act on when we are doing less. I believe that when we feel exhausted or when we're not taking care of ourselves like we should, we limit our access to this creative energy. In contrast, when we surrender and let go, we often almost instantly make room for creativity to come in. The idea that we need to be in a relatively mellow state of mind is something to be mindful of. When we feel stressed or worried, we're less likely to have the ability to be creative or even use all the brain's knowledge and power.

In contrast, when we know that a relaxed state fosters our best work, we can create a better environment for the tasks that matter most. For example, when I have a spacious, clean, and aesthetically pleasing office, not only do I create more powerfully, but I find that I am much more efficient. I can do so much more with less effort. I also seem to be able to do activities in a fraction of the time it takes when my environment is out of sorts and uninspiring.

Once we realize the connection between our environment, our energy, and our abilities, it's easy to maximize productivity. I'm a big proponent of practices like meditation, yoga, walking, and exercise in general, because the time you put into doing those activities will be much more valuable than time you could put into feeling uninspired at a computer or staring at your to-do list. Any activity that helps us to feel better emotionally and physically, or that calms our minds, opens us up to the flow of energy that is always present from whatever spiritual being you believe in.

You may be thinking, "Okay, Leanne, this has happened to me before. I get it. [Or maybe you're still skeptical—that's totally okay too.] But what happens after the divine taps me with some awesome inspiration?" Well, that's up to you. Like attaching feelings to thoughts, we choose to create a positive or negative association with the flow of ideas and creativity that comes from the universe.

For example, when I first had the great idea to start a course called Beautiful Money, I was superexcited about it. I had chosen to make a positive association and had already developed a mental picture of people wanting to take this amazing course. My mind was moving so fast, to map out all the things I wanted to include, that my hands, on the keyboard, literally could not keep up with it. I was that excited. But as I went about the rest of my day, I slowly began to think about the negative things that could happen. I could spend a ton of time, money, and effort on a course that no one was interested in. I could fail. And pretty soon my excitement turned to worry.

This happens to everyone. It's happened to me dozens of times and has likely happened to you multiple times as well. When we have a great idea, we either knock it down right away, by thinking of all the reasons why it couldn't work (making negative associations), or we get really excited for a few days and then start to think about all the ways our idea could fail. We think about all the ways it's not going to work: it's not going to be that great, it's been done before, there's probably a bunch of people who have had this idea before and failed. No matter what the negative inputs are, the result is always the same: a negative association imprinted on our mind. And we know from our previous discussions about how thoughts turn into feelings and leave an imprint on our subconscious that once we've reached this stage it's hard to change our perception of the idea back into something positive.

However, it's important to note that we can use the same tool that works to put a positive spin on our thoughts to attach a positive association to our ideas and inspiration. Doing so creates a pathway in our brain that builds our motivation and allows us to mentally minimize the negative outcomes that could happen. It's very easy to see how we can use disciplined thinking to create a positive association or picture around our ideas as well as our thoughts. Put together, this helps us move from hoping for the best to expecting it—because we're no longer unconsciously labeling everything that comes into our brain as negative.

As I've mentioned before, the key to creating Beautiful Money is to focus on what we do want rather than what we don't. This also applies to what occurs when we have a great idea or are tempted to try something new. We can concentrate on creating a positive association—what we do want—rather than relying on the default mode of the unconscious mind, which is a negative association. Simply put, we need to be conscious about the association and picture we're drawing in our mind—just as we are about attaching feelings to each thought we have. It's a lot easier to change how we think or feel in our conscious mind than to alter a belief that is rooted in our unconscious mind.

WHAT DO YOU REALLY BELIEVE?

A MENTOR ONCE pointed out to me that it's easy to tell what a person believes by the words that person uses in conversations. I use this all the time with my clients. If a client says to me, "I hope this works" or "I'm going to try it," I know that person hasn't truly committed to making a change. His or her unconscious mind hasn't yet made the leap to expecting something different.

This week, examine what you are saying both to yourself and to others. Have you captured that burning desire, that gut energy, to make a change? Or are you still sitting on the fence? If the latter, revisit the tools in step two.

It takes a lot of work to identify the beliefs and habits that are no longer serving us on our path to Beautiful Money and to plant different ideas in our subconscious. But it can be done. Think about growing a plant in your garden. If you feed it negatively, by not giving it enough water and sunlight, it will perish. But given the right conditions, that same plant will grow without any special intervention needed.

Our ideas and belief systems operate the exact same way. If we think of our ideas as seeds, we can treat them the same way. We plant an idea in our subconscious mind, *expect* that idea to grow and develop, and when it does, we can harvest the fruit. It's easy to see how this concept relates to business and our finances. Often when we don't see results right away at work or with a decision surrounding our money, we get nervous. We were *hoping* what we did would work instead of *expecting* it to, so doubt creeps in. Pretty soon we're not as confident about our decision, and then we may decide that the move we made was a mistake and that we should return to the status quo.

However, when we *expect* our choice to be correct and to pay off in the end, we tend to remain confident about our decision and can be more patient waiting for tangible results. This is how we create Beautiful Money. But to have that level of patience and trust, we need to develop a mind-set to support it. That's why we are tackling our mind-set in Week Two, but not taking action until Week Three.

The Beautiful Money
CONFIDENCE BUILDER

WE ALL HAVE fears. Our work is to practice taking action anyway. The challenge we face in our lives is that action is required to create beautiful and fulfilling results. And we often don't act unless we are confident.

Within that lies a great lesson. To gain confidence, we must find the courage to act. If we let fears lead our lives, we will never take action and never develop true self-confidence. But we can take baby steps toward confidence by tuning in to ourselves each and every time we make decisions.

The simple five-step process that follows has helped me tremendously over the years. It's helped me become a person of action even when fear wants to hold me back. I use the steps as my way to gracefully (or as gracefully as possible at the time) face challenges with poise and confidence. With time, this process has helped me grow and strengthen my self-confidence—and with practice it can do the same for you.

Step 1: Sit with the decision and the action your intuition is telling you to take.

Step 2: Clearly state the intention behind the decision or the action you want to take.

Step 3: Let fearful thoughts and feelings come up, but practice detachment. Observe, but don't attach feelings or emotions to what you think. Sit with the decision at hand, and create quiet space to contemplate what your heart wants, not what your head wants.

Step 4: Talk out your situation, thoughts, and feelings with someone you completely trust and admire, who wants you to shine brightly in your life. Be very mindful to select someone you truly admire, who is positive and fabulous. As an alternative, you can use journaling and meditation as a way to get really connected to yourself and the decision at hand. At the end of the day, you already know the answer! If you do talk out your situation with someone, remember to always own your choice. Others can give opinions, but be mindful that only you know the right answer for you. Some decisions you can make quickly, but others take time and space (for example, whether or not to stay in a relationship, to end an unhealthy friendship, or to make a career change).

Step 5: Once you have made your decision, work out an action plan that includes self-care, a fabulous circle of friends, someone you can lean on during the action process (like a mentor or peer or partner), physical movement (like walking, running,

yoga, or dance), and extra personal time. And commit to it. Extra personal time is extremely helpful
during key decision times in your life. This personal
time will help you stay connected to your heart and
your highest self. We will talk more about action
later in the book. For now, just know that taking loving action with intention and awareness is key to
creating Beautiful Money.

THE BEAUTIFUL MONEY MANTRA

As I mentioned before, we all need tools to maintain a positive
mind-set that expects the best. But we also need tools to help us
move forward toward our goals and to help us grow within ourselves to be better every day. That's what creating a Beautiful
Money mantra provides.

Mantras are similar to affirmations in that both allow us to shift
our emotional state and feelings in an abundant direction. Personally, I see mantras more as philosophical statements than as affirmations, which to me are tools of support and encouragement. If we
think of an affirmation as an ego and confidence boost, a mantra is
more like an anthem or a personal mission statement.

Your Beautiful Money mantra should be a statement that's
powerful enough to serve as a motivator. It should challenge you
to act, because its purpose is to help you move in the right direction. Remember that at any given time we are moving either toward our goal or toward what we don't want. Mantras help us stay
on track. Ideally, we want to be constantly learning, in a state of
growth in which we are improving every day. Your Beautiful
Money mantra should be aligned with that ideal.

Here are a few mantras from clients who have taken the course:

- I always speak my truth. I no longer settle for anything less.
- Beauty, abundance, and grace flow my way every day. Every cell of my body reminds me that I deserve the very best.
- I always have more than enough money. I am financially self-sufficient and actively share my wealth both spiritually and monetarily with the world.
- I am more than enough and am exactly where I am supposed to be. I already have all the answers.

To create your own mantra, think about a fear you have that comes up around money. Here's what my clients tend to express:

- Money stresses me out
- I am afraid of not having enough money
- I am afraid of losing money
- I don't have enough time to create wealth
- I am a parent and therefore can't create wealth for myself
- I can't make money
- I am afraid of money
- If I accumulate wealth, I will lose my money or spend it all
- I am afraid to manage money
- I will lose friends if I create wealth for myself
- I will not be aligned spiritually if I create wealth for myself
- I am not worthy of money or wealth
- Wealth will change me for the worse
- I would have to burn myself out to make more money
- I would have to work really hard to make money

- I don't believe I can make more money
- I don't believe I am worthy of wealth
- I would have to live in misalignment to create wealth
- Money is confusing and complicated
- I'm not smart enough to create or manage wealth
- I am not worthy of great abundance
- People with money aren't trustworthy
- I can't create wealth doing what I love
- I am angry at money
- I am destined to be in debt
- I am destined to be broke
- I will always be in debt
- I am always stressed about money
- I will never be wealthy
- Wealthy people are not good people
- If I create wealth, I will be alone
- I am afraid to take care of myself
- I am afraid of success
- I am afraid of failing
- I would have to turn into a workaholic to create wealth
- My circumstances prevent me from creating wealth

Let's pretend that you have an underlying fear that you will never make enough money. You may worry about how hard it is to make money or what would happen if you couldn't work hard enough to pay your bills and support yourself and your family (begging for loans, ending up broke, relying on government hand-outs, becoming homeless—trust me, we become very imaginative when we let our unconscious mind operate unchecked).

What we want to do is spin that fear in a positive direction. This helps us trick our unconscious mind into a new thought pattern. So instead of thinking that money is difficult or hard to make, that you have to burn yourself out to make money, or that you are some-how incapable of generating enough income to support yourself and your family, you could craft a mantra that essentially says the opposite. For example: *I attract money everywhere I go in an easy and flowing way.*

Like affirmations, your Beautiful Money mantra might in the beginning seem a little unrealistic or disingenuous. That's inevitable, because when we begin using these tools, the negative parts of our ego, identity, and self-talk chime in. When this occurs, practice disciplined thinking. Remember that this is what the mantra is for—to change this type of self-doubting reaction. Know and trust and expect that when you use the mantra repeatedly over time, there will come a day when you totally believe it. (And then it's time for a new mantra!)

THE BEAUTIFUL MONEY FLOW

Dream ⟹ Expect ⟹ Act

So how do we actually create what we want? So far this week, I've explained this process in bits and pieces, but now we can put together the whole. There are three steps we take in order to act in alignment with creating Beautiful Money.

First, we *give ourselves permission to dream big.*

We affirm that we are open channels for greatness and inspiration. We allow any source of inspiration and creativity to download into us. We also align our thoughts with our greatest desires. We do our best to align our mind, body, and spirit. This alignment helps us connect to the universal source of inspiration. We take great care of ourselves and acknowledge ourselves as divine and creative beings. We respect our own power and that of the world around us. We practice keeping ourselves as open and flowing as possible, at all times, to sources of inspiration, including the great ideas that come to us in the middle of the night. We also practice aligning the words we speak with our highest selves. Words that feel true, right, and full of energy make up the majority of our vocabulary.

If I'm being honest, I wasn't always the greatest example when it comes to aligning my words with my highest self. For a few years (and two different pregnancies), I let circumstances in my life infuse negative energy into my language. This did not serve me well. I was an emotional mess for longer than I needed to be. A friend and online marketing expert I interviewed during this time said to me, "Sometimes we need to take a little step back to take a big leap forward." This was exactly what I needed to hear. I was able to take a step back, allow the universe to do a little work on my behalf, and get back on track by mindfully choosing words that radiate light, love, and positive energy. It took a little bit of time, but I was able to change how I talked to myself and the world around me, which then helped me get back into alignment. With experience, I have also learned to forgive myself for being a hot mess every once in a while!

Second, we *expect greatness*.

We stop *hoping* for good things to happen. Instead, we use tools to build up confidence in ourselves, reframing our neurological patterns so we come to expect the best rather than focusing on bad things that could happen. I believe building up strong confidence is the key to developing the ability to expect that our dreams are in the process of becoming reality. You might need to lean on others (those you deeply love and trust) to help you muster up the belief that you can do anything and everything you set your mind to.

A practice I have is to remember a sentence one of my mentors told me: "Why would you have the dream in the first place if it wasn't meant for you?" I stick with this when

I need more confidence. In order to act on and create our greatest life, we must divorce from hoping for what we desire most. We must learn to expect our desires to be fulfilled (even if we are a little rusty in the beginning).

Third—and this is what we'll cover next week—we *act*.

We use all the positivity we've created in the first two steps to move toward our goals and to grow ourselves even more.

It's easier to be conscious of the flow of dreaming big ——➤ expectation ——➤ action when we know what we truly want and how we want to get there. We can focus on creating a positive association with the ideas that the divine has given us and begin to avoid the negative, limiting feelings that bubble up when we start to doubt ourselves.

Take a moment to think about where you've succeeded and where you have failed in the past. Did you begin those journeys expecting to win? Or did you engage with an initial seed of doubt in your gut? With the help of hindsight, it's easy to see how this universal flow affected your life before you even heard of Beautiful Money!

The truth is, most people wish positively (I wish I had enough money to be financially free) but think negatively: What would I do with my days if I didn't work? How would I manage that kind of money? I've never known anything other than living paycheck to paycheck, so clearly I'm not equipped to be financially stable. There must be something wrong with me. . . . It's easy to see where this example is headed.

The truth is that the vast majority of people don't attract abundance because they get in their own way. Most people forget that openness and flexibility are keys to wealth. We all accidentally let our egos lead from time to time, and we forget that being coachable and open to new information is part of creating Beautiful Money and cultivating visionary leadership.

We all have something to learn—always. I have found that many people say they are coachable and ready to create wealth, but this proves to be true only for advice or opinions these individuals agree with. The truth is, the more energetic space that gets clogged up by beliefs, thoughts, and habits that aren't aligned with health, wealth, and happiness, the less room there is for wealth to move into our lives.

Often our unconscious, negative thoughts can be the limiting factor, not our ability to actually make or manage money. One of my dearest mentors taught me that great wealth isn't really about learning more; it's about letting go! This is still one of my most cherished pieces of advice.

Every time I have let go of old habits, thoughts, or patterns that were no longer serving me, my income has jumped! My former ways were clogging up my cells and taking up serious space in my life. There was just no room for bigger, brighter, and lighter ways of living! That's why letting go and the act of cleansing have become my favorite pastimes. It isn't always easy (especially when it involves being hurt or heartbroken), but it is simple!

If there's one message I'd like for you to take from this week, it's that when we hope for one thing but expect the opposite, it's our expectation that becomes reality. We can hope all we want, but hope isn't enough to move us toward action. We need to be aligned emotionally with our goals and our core values. We need to expect to win at our lives. Then and only then will we be powerfully self-motivated to act in the direction of our dreams.

To truly attract abundance, we need to know what we want, to be clear about why we want it, to expect to receive what we want, and then to take the necessary actions to get there. In Week Three, we'll put your new mind-set to the test by acting on the clarity and focus we've developed thus far.

WEEK THREE

WEEK THREE

Become an Action Heroine

To act in alignment with Beautiful Money, we must be clear about what we want and why we want it. And to make gorgeous space for the great, we have to cleanse our lives of everything that's not working for us. In the past two weeks, we've done exactly that.

In this third week of the program, what we'll learn gets really juicy! We will use the foundation of truth (our WHY, our mantra, and our newfound belief in our own selves) that we've created to define our goals—financially, emotionally, spiritually—as well as to build habits and practices we can use on a daily basis that align our time and effort with what we want to achieve.

Step one will show you how to move more easily into action by creating clarity. By becoming crystal clear about when you want to be financially and emotionally free, and by setting a realistic goal for what you'd like your net worth to be this time next year, you will develop a loving sense of urgency for getting it done.

Step two will help you increase your income and meet the goals you set in the first step by aligning your time with actions that actually create profit. These are your Beautiful Money activities. You will want to pay extra loving attention to this section. Focusing more of your time on Beautiful Money activities will not only bring you more joy but will also bring greater wealth into your life. This section will answer the all-important question: How do I make more money?

Finally, in step three we will address the practical aspects of money management, from budgeting and different ways of creating income to establishing and automating strategies for saving and investing money that will, over time, create holistic wealth. In this section, I show why and how it's the little things we do with great care and consistency that create great wealth in the long run.

Unlike in previous weeks, this week we don't concentrate as much on our beliefs. We do, however, continue to pay close attention to our internal landscape. Remember that creating Beautiful Money is, first and foremost, an inside job. Once we get clear, we can focus on external activities and habits that will move more money our way.

Our goal this week is to shift our attention to how we show up in our everyday lives. More specifically, we'll look at the very practical ways we behave around money. How do we create income? Do we spend our time in ways that either waste what we have or neglect what we could create? What habits hold us back from our next stage of wealth and abundance?

The exercises and lessons this week will improve your habits and renovate your routine so you can move toward your next level of personal growth, fulfillment, and abundance on a daily basis. In essence, this week sets you up for success creating Beautiful Money.

STEP ONE:
ACT AS IF (FAILING IS IMPOSSIBLE)

A big part of my business is mentoring others who are on the path to Beautiful Money. After more than a decade of working with well-intentioned clients, I've learned that most of us don't truly know how to balance action and allowing. Most of the time, we either take scattered action without a clear goal in mind or find ourselves in a state of waiting for everything to be perfect before we take action.

Most people either overvalue action or undervalue it. What does this mean? Imagine a time in your life when your gut was telling you to slow down and enjoy the ride but you chose to burn the midnight oil, overfill your to-do list, and multitask like a machine. I know this has happened to me. When we run our lives this way and mindlessly burn ourselves out while focused on our to-do lists, we often achieve less than we would if we did nothing. Why? Because real achievement is not about just any action; it's about well-thought-out, focused, and intentional action. The plans we make and execute must be clear, focused, and totally aligned if we want to achieve mind-blowing greatness. Success is not about luck; it's about clarity, focus, and alignment.

I have found, through my years of mentoring, that many people don't act because of fear. Some are afraid to fail, while others are afraid of their own power and what would happen if they did succeed. One of my mentors, Tama Kieves, once said, "You're so good at something you don't even like. Imagine how extraordinary you'll be at something you love." That sentence changed my life forever.

Failure happens, and we will all experience it. But consider failure as a fabulous learning opportunity and beautiful bump along the road to making your dreams a reality. We always transform after adversity, emerging stronger, more powerful, and more resilient.

When we unconsciously embrace the "burnout" philosophy of life, days, months, and even years get stolen from us because we're chasing a never-ending to-do list. This is where things really get messy. When we live on overdrive, we are disconnected not only from our bodies and selves but from the world around us. For me, this happened when I chose to be in insane overdrive during my second pregnancy. I ignored my intuitive nudges and bulldozed my way into a big, hot mess.

I basically did everything I'm telling you not to do throughout this book! But that experience was valuable because I learned that when we ignore our intuition and choose to be in overdrive, it may seem like we are moving forward, but the opposite is true.

This is one principle of the *Tao Te Ching* that I love: "The Tao does nothing yet leaves nothing undone."[14] This principle reminds me that when I feel frazzled, hyper, and out of sync with myself, doing nothing is always the best option. Taking a day off, going to a yoga class, or going for a walk will be far more productive in the long run. Why? Because when we act from a place of inner chaos, tension, or ego-centered emotion, we are in a state of forcing. And when we're in that state of pushing to make things happen, the flow of divine energy and creativity is blocked, and projects certainly don't get done drama-free. Our cells tense up, our bodies stiffen, and we lose connection. Essentially, we make whatever we're trying to do harder than it should be.

Here's why: taking action without a clear intention in mind (or with an entire to-do list in mind) inevitably leads to stress and unhappiness because we are living somewhere other than now (we are disconnected). Our actions aren't aligned with our four pillars or what we truly aim to do. Soon we end up chasing money and find ourselves back where we started, feeling like a hamster on a wheel. Before I discovered my own path to Beautiful Money, I was totally living that way.

Beautiful Money Tip

EMEMBER THAT BEAUTIFUL Money is a process and an evolution. You will often feel like you're taking a step backward. Sometimes a small step backward (and it might feel like a big one) is a divinely timed necessity for your upcoming big leap forward.

The flip side of overvaluing action and ending up burned out is undervaluing action by waiting for something or someone to come and take the lead for you. I call this "messing with momentum." This often happens to individuals who are very creative but tend to chase perfection. When we wait for everything to be perfect and all the stars to align before making a move, we aren't acknowledging, or prioritizing, the importance of just doing it. I know a client is in the "messing with momentum" state when she says something like "When I get to my perfect weight, I will start dressing better," or "When I'm done with my maternity leave, I will start taking care of myself again," or "When I'm out of debt, I'll start my dream business."

A client may say to me, "I don't want to launch my website until . . . ," or "I want everything to be just right before. . . ." Regardless of what follows, the beginnings of those statements tell me (and the universe) that my client is waiting for perfection. But even more important, he or she clearly has not digested the simple truth that we must move toward the direction of our dreams today.

Think of it this way: Time is our most precious resource. We can never get our time back. Only the present moment is guaranteed. It is our utmost responsibility to act in an aligned, abundant, and authentic way whenever possible. Chasing perfection wastes time and energy.

Imagine waking up twenty years from now still waiting for your website to be perfect to launch or with a creative pursuit lying unseen in a drawer somewhere. No one wants that. I am a big advocate of taking action with a loving sense of urgency. Don't let the urge for perfection steal your time, your beauty, and your creativity.

Instead, trust that nothing will ever totally be ready, nothing will ever be exact, nothing will ever be complete, but what you do offer the world is always perfectly imperfect. The world wants you to share your beauty and your gifts today. All you have is right now, and right now is the perfect time for action.

There will never be a better time to start taking action than today. Actually, yesterday would have been better, but remember, we are always exactly where we are supposed to be. Alignment (which you built and practiced over the past two weeks) combined with action is the only way to attract and create Beautiful Money. Once we're aligned, action with a loving sense of urgency is the next step to achieving holistic wealth. This piece is what I feel is missing from most people's lives. The brilliant Dr. Wayne Dyer once said, "Stop acting as if life is a rehearsal. . . . The past is over and gone. The future is not guaranteed."[15] It's easy to see how people can live their entire lives in preparation for the big show, the big day, the moment when all extenuating circumstances and risk will be eliminated, when success is a sure thing.

But guess what? That's never going to happen. When we wait *until*—until things are perfect, until we've saved enough money, until we have a six-figure income, until our kids are grown, until we get married, until we are more fit or focused, or until whatever benchmark or status or goal will mean we're ready—wealth and abundance simply cannot reach us, and we've wasted that precious time waiting for . . . what exactly?

The great taps of the universe are turned on, and Beautiful Money is flowing *now*. If you're waiting for trivial things to be perfect before you act, the universe simply won't deliver Beautiful Money to you. The universe likes speed. In my opinion, waiting and hesitation cost us the opportunity to create tremendous wealth and abundance.

This is the true cost of seeking perfection.

Beautiful Money Tip

I HAVE WORKED WITH dozens of clients who want to start a business but who hesitate to launch it publicly for weeks, months, years. These clients tend to make excuses like "The time isn't right," "What will people think?," "My business plan isn't finished," or, my favorite, "I'm going to wait until. . . ."

As soon as those words reach me, I know that deep down my client needs a gentle and loving reminder that he or she is worthy of great success and abundance *now*. At its root, perfectionism is about not feeling good enough. I recently watched a conversation between Oprah Winfrey and Dr. Brené Brown (a professor at the University of Houston who has spent the last decade studying vulnerability and courage) on the TV show *Super Soul Sunday*, during which Dr. Brown explained that perfectionism is not about striving for excellence; it's a way of thinking or feeling that says, "If I look perfect, do it perfect, work perfect, and live perfect, I can avoid or minimize shame, blame, and judgment." In response, Oprah said, "Perfectionism is the ultimate fear."[16] And that is so true!

When we hesitate or put achieving our goals on hold "until," it's a reflection of a voice or belief deep inside us that's saying, "I'm not good enough so I'm going to wait until I feel like I'm good enough." But guess what? The only thing that's going to make you feel like you are

worthy is telling that voice to shove it and taking a courageous leap anyway.

Taking that big leap will be a little scary but completely
exhilarating too. To muster the courage to move, we
might need to close our eyes, take a deep breath, tune
out the inner ego voice, and let our heart move us forward. When we stop for a moment of stillness, with an
ear toward our hearts, that's where we find courage.

So if you are a recovering perfectionist, joke about being a control freak, or know that you're a little type A, acknowledging your fear is an important element to work
on. Luckily, this is an easy task. Tell your inner haters and
doubters no—as many times as you need to. Be kind to
yourself. You wouldn't let another person talk to you that
way, so why are you allowing yourself to be your own
worst enemy? Talk back. Stop being your own bully. Be
your own best friend. Practicing compassion and kindness and being your own cheerleader, instead of your
own victim or bully, is the best way to build confidence
and break out of the perfectionist mind-set that's holding
you back from abundance right now. Yes, this work is
scary—but you're worth it.

Balancing action and allowing is essential to creating Beautiful
Money. We must be mindful of forcing action or we risk creating
the chaos that led us to want to change our lives in the first place.
But we also can't allow our fears and past beliefs to stick us in an
eternal waiting room where we let days and months go by without
doing anything to make our dreams a reality.

We need to create action with a loving sense of urgency, to
move our lives forward with positive momentum. This, and only
this, puts us in a place where we can receive and welcome holistic
abundance with open arms.

YOUR CELEBRATION DATES

If gaining momentum is key to creating Beautiful Money, then we need to know what we are moving toward. This step is all about beginning to define, financially, where you are headed on your Beautiful Money journey and ensuring that what you document gets done. (We'll sharpen and define broader goals next week.)

It's great to dream, visualize, and imagine, but if you never put your plans on paper, your dreams just won't come true (at least not in a timely way). Writing down key dates, goals, and plans on paper will absolutely create magical momentum in your life.

I like to explain how this works as if it's an old game show. There are two doors. Behind door number one is you choosing to keep your dreams to yourself and locked up in your mind. Behind door number two is a different story, in which you clearly define your greatest desires, dreams, and plans with purpose and burning desire, first in your head and then on paper, the old-fashioned way, with a pen.

If you choose door number one, you essentially leave your life up to chance. Your goals and dreams may come to fruition but it might take a decade or two (or three), whereas if you choose door number two, you are tapping into the magic that occurs as your pen strokes the paper with your dreams and desires. It's as if each letter contains within it a magical life force that expands beyond space and time. In order to create Beautiful Money, we need to choose door number two.

We begin by remembering the feelings we get when we celebrate something fabulous in our lives. How did you feel the last time you celebrated something near and dear to your heart? It's time to establish and document key dates for your freedom. Every date you write down will be worthy of celebrating once achieved.

And since we have already learned that expectation is one of the keys to creating Beautiful Money, let's start to put ourselves into a celebratory emotional state now, since we know the party is on its way! Remember that celebrating every inch of success along the way will only bring more success. Consider celebrating your very own gratitude practice for your life.

I used to consciously choose to avoid celebrating successes. I actually felt bad celebrating. But then I thought: What's up with that? My rationale used to be that I was a humble person who recognized that greater forces were at work in my successes and that it was egotistical to celebrate them. But as decades went by, I felt a deep sense of grief. I started to recognize that I felt profoundly sad for not joyfully thanking the universe for the experiences I had cocreated. Funny enough, my husband (and my greatest teacher) used to be the same way. Now that we are in our forties, we have grandly proclaimed to each other and the universe that celebrating is our new gratitude practice! And, not to toot our own horns (joke intended), we are becoming really great at it!

We will create celebration dates for financial freedom, debt freedom, mortgage freedom—and for any other money goal that you had in mind when you bought this book. We'll also reexamine the net worth you calculated in Week One and set a goal for the figure you want to see when you make that same calculation in a year.

Attaching a date to your financial goals may seem scary or intimidating, but remember that there will never be a day when everything is perfect and aligned, when the universe calls down from on high that it's time to achieve your next level. The universe helps us whenever we choose to act on our mission and our goals by actually committing to doing. Taking action—even just a simple act like figuring out where you're headed—might feel risky, but it will put you on the path for great change and abundance in your life. So let's get started.

In all the exercises in this step, we want to choose dates and financial benchmarks that feel right to us. There's no "correct" or "incorrect" answer; the goal is to feel slightly uncomfortable yet challenged by what you've set out to achieve. A financial freedom date that makes us so stressed we feel like throwing up or that is set so far in the future that we can't even imagine living at that point in time (say, in 2100) simply will not be effective.

Beautiful Money Tip

*I*T'S BEST TO turn your practical, pragmatic brain off when creating goals and defining your freedom dates. This helps you tune in to your deepest desires and focus on the future, instead of getting caught up in fear, doubt, and worry about all the steps your journey may require.

The first goal I'd like for you to define is your **debt-free date**. When it comes to creating Beautiful Money, nothing pulls us down more than heavy debt. Owing money creates negative energy, sucks our life force, and weighs us down in life. Debt doesn't have to be huge to make you feel weighted down. Debts of any kind draw us down to the ground when what we want, and are meant to do, is to fly. Heavy debt is the minus sign that shows up in our accounting and makes us want to barf. This is the debt that has accumulated from our former life chasing money, valuing success more than our health, expressing our emotions during shopping sprees, spending just to keep up with the Joneses, and attempting to be a collector of more stuff than our neighbors.

Obviously, by this definition, consumer and credit card debt is a perfect example of a heavy debt load. Money that you owe friends or family members, bills that you have nothing to show for, tax debt, even an outstanding loan that you dread paying month after month should all be included in this category.

That being said, what financial advisers would label as "good debt"—like student loans and income-generating properties—could also fall into this category if you feel like they are a burden financially or emotionally. Mortgages, car payments, and student loans are technically debt, but the energy associated with that debt varies. For example, a real estate agent in a prestigious neighborhood may need a luxury car to successfully accumulate clients. Racking up student debt that financed an Ivy League MBA or medical school or a degree that led to your dream job or career is usually worth it.

This book does not take a black-and-white approach to categorizing debt as good or bad. Instead, it asks you to take a deeper look at your debt, the intention behind that debt, and the emotional energy associated with it.

Consider this: Is debt really "good" if it has resulted in feeling unwell, not sleeping at night, or daily worry about how much money is in your bank accounts? And is debt really "bad" if it's helped you to succeed? Debt that has helped you grow a business or build a career shouldn't be seen as toxic or dirty. If your debt has helped you leverage yourself into making more money, that's amazing! Using other people's money to grow your empire and build a legacy is part of the Beautiful Money plan. What isn't pretty is debt that makes you feel unwell, lose sleep at night, or makes you feel anxious, nervous, or nauseous. This debt should be eliminated with as much loving sense of urgency as possible. That's what our debt-free celebration date is for: to clear that debt and shed that load from your life forever.

*Y*EARS AGO, MY dear friend and colleague Julie encouraged me to buy my first luxury car. I told her I was totally happy with my six-year-old Jeep Liberty. My SUV wasn't luxurious, but it functioned well and I loved it. Julie explained that because I was beginning a new chapter as a lifestyle and wealth mentor, it was important for me to feel abundant. She knew that deep down I was living within my comfort zone and had a few scarcity beliefs of my own creeping around in my mind.

Julie challenged me to step up and step out of my comfort zone. She said, "Leanne, you are great with money. You can afford the dream car you have on your vision board. What are you waiting for? Go buy it today!"

So I called a friend who I knew was just about to buy her dream car and told her that I would love to chat with her car dealer. My dream car at the time was a black BMW X6. She put me in touch with the dealer she had worked with, and we both bought our dream cars that same week! It was scary but so much fun.

I am a practical girl and ultraresponsible (sometimes to a fault), so going out and buying a luxury car was not something I was emotionally prepared for—but I did it anyway!

I needed to be pushed out of my comfort zone. And because it is important to be clear about how you will serve the world in exchange for the Beautiful Money you desire, I chose to give my Jeep away. I could have sold it, but it felt so much better to gift it to family. Hello, Beautiful Money in action! I took out a loan to purchase my new car but didn't feel any bad energy associated with the debt. I could afford it, and I believed that the purchase was worth it.

My first choice would usually be to be my own bank and have the money saved up prior to purchasing a car. But in this case my passive weekly income far exceeded my expenses (even when I included my weekly savings). I was also single and I decided to create a stretch goal of having the car loan repaid in less than two years. Because my car was used for business, there were also some tax benefits.

Buying a car isn't traditionally considered good debt, but in my case it made me happy (I bought my dream car), it helped me attract even more business and clients, and I committed to having the entire debt paid off in two years. I purchased the car, put the debt-free date for my car in my calendar, and moved forward with excellence.

The day I went into the bank to pay off my debt in full, the bank manager smiled and said, "Wow! You must feel amazing!" And I did. I had made a commitment to myself to budget and to save enough income to pay it off in two years, and I made it happen. Years later, I sold the car for more than its market value. I loved that car and it served me well.

A classic example of what I call "heavy debt" is a credit card for which you've been paying the minimum every month but have neglected to see how much interest you're paying. Could you make a bigger payment and pay off the balance sooner? Do you even know the interest rates for your credit cards? What would it take for you to eliminate all your credit card debt? How soon could you pay off your loans? If you know deep down in your gut that you could do more about any of your debts, write down a date that feels challenging but not overwhelming.

When I set my first debt-free date, I prioritized a ten-thousand-dollar loan I had received from my mom. I had used the money for something beneficial—the down payment on a property—but simply having an outstanding debt with her affected my energy. I am a Virgo and need to feel clean and light. Although I had other debt, paying my mom back first felt best. I chose to prioritize paying back that loan before tackling my consumer debt. While it would have saved me money to pay off my credit cards first, I knew I wouldn't stop worrying until I'd paid my mom back. In other words, if you can earn back some much-needed spiritual interest by tackling an emotionally toxic debt first, doing so will be more beneficial than any financial gain.

I believe how you feel is an important factor to consider when paying back your debt, because lightening my emotional load raised my state of vibration. When I cleansed my body of the stress and tension of owing my mom money, my creative juices instantly began to flow again. This greatly enhanced my ability and power to create more Beautiful Money in my life.

When you are aligned with yourself and a purpose, anything is possible. When you feel clean and clear, you feel like you can take on the world. This emotional state can move mountains. In my experience, every time I shed an emotional load, my income grows exponentially (not just a few percentage points).

So although I am responsible and practical, and almost always suggest paying back debt with the highest interest first, I do take a holistic approach to debt repayment. When you clear up a situation that is causing stress and tension in your body, you improve your emotional vibration and your ability to magnetically attract money.

So any bill that makes you feel depressed or anxious should be considered and tackled first in your holistic wealth plan. One of my clients, Amy, had substantial student-loan debt. Although she felt relatively neutral about the $250 she paid toward the loans she had accumulated during her undergraduate education, the $400 payment she made every month for her graduate-degree loans made her feel crappy. Amy confided that she had run up those loans unnecessarily and that her graduate education wasn't really worth the money she had borrowed. Making that payment each and every month was simply a reminder of how irresponsible she had been. So we figured out how to prioritize paying off her graduate school loans. By adding an extra $100 to her monthly payment, Amy was able to decrease the amount of interest she was paying on what she felt was bad debt. Although she wasn't going to pay off all of her student loans, she could see an end in sight for the specific loan that carried negative energy. Creating a debt-free date for that particular loan changed the way Amy felt about making that payment every month and helped her to feel like she was no longer paying for her past mistakes, emotionally or financially.

Beautiful Money Tip

IF YOU ARE in a debt jam, there is no better tonic than to commit to learning what you need to learn and doing what you need to do to get out of it yourself. How else will you fully learn the lessons and strategies you need to learn?

In my opinion, figuring out how to resolve your own heavy debt is one of the best self-esteem courses ever. What better way to show yourself that you can do it and you are worthy? Imagine how you would feel once you got yourself out of debt. Like a Beautiful Money maven! True leadership is developed when we commit to excellence when we're in a jam, not when everything is going great.

Resolving your own debt may not be easy, and you

may feel like giving up, but persist. Developing the habit of persistence and self-discipline is absolutely mandatory if you are committed to Beautiful Money.

But please know: although I admire those who have taken the tough road and dug themselves out of a debt jam, I do believe that some situations are best solved by declaring bankruptcy. If your credit card bills are truly overwhelming, and you spend every moment of your life feeling like barfing, filing for bankruptcy may be an option. As personal finance expert Liz Weston explains in *The 10 Commandments of Money*, "If your toxic debt would take more than five years to pay off you may want to consider your alternatives. Why five years? Because that's as long as you would have to remain on a repayment plan with a Chapter 13 bankruptcy; after that, most remaining unsecured debt, such as credit cards and medical bills, would be erased. If you qualified for a Chapter 7 bankruptcy, your debt might be erased in a few months without a repayment plan."[17]

Obviously, bankruptcy isn't ideal for everyone, and I would make it your last resort, especially if you have significant assets. If you are reading this and have contemplated bankruptcy, it's important to consult with an attorney to assess your current financial situation and see whether bankruptcy is right for you. In the United States, the National Association of Consumer Bankruptcy Attorneys (NACBA) offers a search tool on its website (www .nacba.org/find-an-attorney) that can help you find an expert in your area.

Your debt-free date should have the same power and promise for you as it did for Amy and for me. If you feel like you are drowning in a sea of bills, this date should be a light showing you the way out. As a general rule, I'd like you to remain consumer-debt-free as much as possible while attracting Beautiful Money. If you're not there now, eliminating debt should be a primary goal. If you can stay dirty-debt-free, you will allow your mind, body, and spirit to be free from the energetic heaviness associated with bad debt. The lighter you keep your mind, body, and spirit, the more powerful your ability to create and attract Beautiful Money.

Before moving forward, I want you to take a moment and a breath.

I want you to affirm your intention out loud and on paper.

What is your debt-free date?

Write it down now.

The next financial goal I'd like for you to set is your **mortgage-free date**.

I used to dislike and fear all debt. Debt made me very emotional. I saw any debt as bad—regardless of the details, like its purpose, interest rates, payment structure, and potential equity. To me, all debt was the same: dirty! It was all bad. And all of it needed to be paid off right away. I admit that I still have some lingering emotions about debt, but I have learned to take a more neutral approach. My mind knows that leveraging other people's money to create an empire is how wealth is created, but my body still dislikes the feeling of being in debt. I get around this by keeping my bad debt to almost zero. My accountant has been helpful in reminding me during my Beautiful Money practice that some debts, like a mortgage, can be beneficial when structured properly and balanced with other investments in my portfolio. That's why mortgages and other positive debts like student loans aren't lumped in with the junk debts that make us feel bad and can lower our net worth. I overpaid my mortgage for a year while interest rates were very low. The payments and interest rate were completely reasonable, but I bent over backward to pay three times what I owed each month in an attempt to be mortgage-free within just two to three years. When it came time to file taxes, my accountant pointed out that I could have been investing the money I was overpaying. Instead, I ended up paying more taxes (because I'm self-employed, I had to receive a larger salary to cover these extra mortgage payments, which resulted in more money owing to the government).

Basically, I was shooting myself in the foot financially. I chose to listen to the expert, started investing the amount I was overpaying, and realigned my mortgage-free date to be more realistic and beneficial to my entire financial portfolio. This was holistic wealth planning in action.

Don't get me wrong. I am all for being mortgage-free as quickly as possible, but there are often several factors to consider in the long term and where tax strategies are concerned. I realized that I was obsessively paying down my mortgage at the expense of other areas of my life, and my lifestyle was based completely on fear. I was more afraid of debt and not having enough than I was focused on creating a healthy financial landscape.

My accountant suggested that I put my money elsewhere while interest rates were low, and I agreed. He suggested investing this money and building up my cash flow. I had never thought of that! At the time, building up my liquid cash assets was the smartest and most holistic plan.

Because of my fear of debt, my mind saw only the big, fat amount I owed, and I became fully consumed with paying it off instead of considering my wealth plan from a holistic perspective. I neglected what was financially smart, because of my own fear. This is an example of why it's so important to tune in to your emotional state as you create your empire. You will need a great team of experts to help you along your journey. Women especially can get extra-emotional about money, and having experts who aren't emotionally invested in your situation can be very beneficial. Make sure you wholeheartedly trust the people you hire or work with, though. Be diligent and responsible, and interview experts to ensure you have the right people in place for your situation and personality. If something or someone doesn't feel right, trust your gut.

Many books and advisers say it's best to be entirely debt-free. But that's not always the case. If there is a lot of time left on a mortgage with low interest rates, it may be better to make slightly accelerated payments (to ensure you are digging into getting that principal paid down) and use any extra money to invest in additional properties or other areas. My husband and I like investing in real estate but, again, it is important to assess what wealth vehicles fit best for you. The same rule applies to other forms of debt that are traditionally categorized as "good."

Beautiful Money Tip

REMEMBER, WHAT CAN be classified as "good" or "bad" debt is up to you and how you feel about it. For example, many financial experts would consider a mortgage bad debt, but my husband and I have strategically turned our home loans and real estate into wealth generators in the past. That strategy requires moving every few years, and that's not for everyone. Renovations, and always looking for the next place, can leave some people feeling anxious and ungrounded.

As a mom, I am finally ready to settle into a long-term cozy home. My husband and I have decided that moving our principal residence and renovating homes is no longer part of our Beautiful Money journey.

Remember, practicing Beautiful Money requires both

inner and outer alignment. What served us well in the past may not be true today. That's why Ric and I have decided that moving every few years (because money you generate on your principal residence is tax-free—hello!) is no longer an aligned activity for us as parents and the leaders of a family of six. We will always be on the lookout for amazing "Zenscapes" (what we call land and properties we want to purchase as part of our family legacy and for friends and family to use), but moving every few years is no longer healthy for us. We need a home, not just a profitable house. So while we wouldn't have prioritized or celebrated a mortgage-free date in the past, now we do. We also like to keep the mortgage on our principal residence well under what we can afford, so we can pay it off in a few years (and have lots of equity to further invest).

At the end of the day, if your debt is helping you generate more long-term wealth, that is amazing! If your debt is making you feel nauseated and keeping you broke, it's time to commit to getting it out of your life. (We'll talk more about money management strategies later on this week. It's also smart to consult with an independent financial adviser to address your specific situation.)

I'm all for living luxuriously if you have the means but not if your lifestyle is a facade that you cannot afford or that doesn't serve you well. At the end of the day, a philosophy of always living below your means is a great one. Saving more and spending less will help you sleep wealthy and healthy. It's not about scarcity; it's about living peacefully and joyfully. It's about having a confident smile on your face when a bill comes in because you have more than enough money at the end of the month.

If you have a stunning net worth and a healthy daily dose of cash flow, then go for Dior! But if not, Target is totally fine. I promise. The same goes for houses. We don't need thousands of square feet to be happy.

Before moving forward, I want you to take a moment and a breath.

I want you to affirm your intention out loud and on paper.

What is your mortgage-free date, if you have one?

Write it down now.

Next, we'll figure out when to celebrate your **financial freedom**.

Imagine a lifestyle in which you don't have to work but you love to create. Imagine having a healthy dose of daily cash flow that covers all your expenses and your lifestyle whether you choose to work or to take a monthlong sabbatical with your family.

Imagine a lifestyle in which you fully own your time and your day planner, and no one but you is in charge of how you spend each day. Imagine a lifestyle in which health, creativity, and family activities take precedence over anything else. Imagine a lifestyle in which you live each day out of inspiration and not obligation. When we are constantly chasing money and living paycheck to paycheck, it seems impossible to achieve this level of financial freedom. But I am here to tell you that it is absolutely possible. If I can do it, you can do it!

When I was twenty-eight, I decided to set my thirty-third birthday as the day I wanted to be financially free. And I did it. (I'll explain how later on.) But when I initially made that goal, I wondered if I could actually do it. I knew I was relatively low maintenance, that I didn't spend a ton of money, and that I had given myself five years to figure out how to earn and save enough to live on. That math and path worked for me, but it may be different for you, depending on your income, responsibilities, and lifestyle. I wasn't married and didn't have kids when I set this goal, so a five-year plan seemed reasonable and exciting to me.

Writing down the exact date that you will become financially free may seem daunting or even impossible. That's because it's a big and audacious goal, especially if you don't earn a lot of money, are swimming in debt, or have always lived paycheck to paycheck (or, like many of us, all of the above). Every single time I teach my Beautiful Money course, there's a student or two who hesitates to pick a date.

Beautiful Money Tip

I LOVE THE IDEA of picking a day that has emotional significance as your financial-freedom date. Birthdays, anniversaries, or any day that has special meaning for you can become a powerful reminder and an incentive to keep moving forward no matter what. If you know you will feel more inspired and challenged if you accomplish your goal by your twentieth, thirtieth, fortieth, fiftieth, sixtieth, or any other birthday, go for it!

Work with your personality. I like a challenge and work well with a healthy dose of pressure, so I tend to love a little bit of a time crunch. But this tendency has backfired at times when my desire for achieving a specific goal came at the expense of practicing patience. The result was a tail-chasing action bender. I have become so much better at listening to my body, though my old patterns of achieving at all costs peek back in every once in a while.

A loving sense of urgency, with a healthy dose of patience, is my new mantra and should be yours too.

But, like waiting for perfection, not writing down a date when you will become financially free affirms to the universe that you are noncommittal and undecided. The universe is always watching, listening, and waiting for you to become crystal clear so it can lend a hand. Essentially, when you choose your date for financial freedom and write it down, your next step is to get busy expecting that it's on its way. Your work is then to act in alignment with that expectation. To be financially free requires you to manage your money well and to respect it. I'll show you how to do that later in this week.

Like the path to Beautiful Money in general, how you reach financial freedom is dependent on your deepest desires and your level of commitment. The equation for calculating net worth might be the same for everyone, but every journey is uniquely precious. My friend Bill needed to earn fifteen hundred dollars a week to save enough money over the course of a few years to become financially free and live the lifestyle he truly desired. If you live in a city or another area where the cost of living is higher, your expenses will likely be higher, so it is important that your plan accommodates them. On the flip side, if you have a spouse with residual income or a well-paying job, you may need less time and effort to reach your goal. Teamwork is a gift and an asset!

But no matter how soon or how far away the date you choose, the important part of this exercise is to choose a date and commit to it wholeheartedly. Whether your date is near or far, your homework will be to make sure that deep and exciting feeling in your gut (also known as burning desire) remains present and active. If and when you feel like it's fizzling out, you should spend extra time that day visualizing, affirming, and gazing at your big and bright vision board. Being aligned with a clear intention and taking action toward that intention is what signals to the universe that you are ready to cocreate and actively make your dreams a reality.

Keep in mind that financial freedom doesn't necessarily mean retirement. Some of us may choose to work only part time once the monthly bills are taken care of. But for others (like me) who love their work and find purpose in it, financial freedom might just be another step toward a broader goal of helping others or benefiting the world. The sooner we get our financial, emotional, and physical needs met and organized, the sooner we can dive into that great, adventurous, and meaningful state of aliveness. When our financial obligations and responsibilities are taken care of while we are sleeping or doing other things, we can spend more time being a contagious ball of beaming inspiration for others. Many people spend their entire lives sorting and managing drama, stressing over finances, and numbing emotional disease.

In contrast, the Beautiful Money program challenges you to step into your greatness in this very moment (regardless of your age or your situation). This very instant is the most precious and energetic moment you have. Feel whatever you feel and let go of whatever you need to let go of. It's time to fully experience every inch of what life has to offer and every emotion that comes with it.

Before moving forward, I want you, just as we did with your debt-free and mortgage-free dates, to take a moment and a breath.

I want you to affirm your intention out loud and on paper.

When do you want to celebrate financial freedom?

Write that date down now.

You may also have other **abundance dates.**

Perhaps you want to quit the nine-to-five and launch a more entrepreneurial business, or you dream (like me) of a vacation home on a Caribbean island or (like Ric) of having the funds available to record an album at the top studio in Nashville. If you have a dream that involves a financial benchmark or goal—who doesn't?—*now* is the time to pick a date when you will achieve that dream.

As with financial freedom, setting the right date to achieve your next level of abundance really depends on your unique circumstances and what you're setting out to achieve. For example, I worked with a client named Allison whose dream was to purchase a home on an island in Puget Sound. She had her dream all planned out: her family would vacation there a few weeks a year, and the rest of the time she would rent it out, creating passive income while building equity. Allison lived near the islands, but to make her dream practical and realistic, she would need to buy a different car.

So when we did this exercise, I asked Allison to create two different abundance dates: a date when she would have enough money saved to purchase a new car with cash (so she wouldn't go into debt), and a date when she would be able to make a substantial down payment on a property. The first abundance date (for the car) was about six months away, and the second (for the property) was two years away. Although Allison had been thinking about her dream for years, she admitted to me that she hadn't taken a single step toward making it a reality, nor had she ever written down her financial goals on paper. Writing down the dates helped her to solidify her feeling that getting the house and car was aligned with what she wanted, and enabled her to actually save money to get there in a more flowing and graceful way. Now, three years later, she and her family love their getaway.

BEAUTIFUL MONEY MATH

So you've set your freedom dates, but you may still be wondering how the heck to make this abundance happen while paying your bills. The path to achieving holistic abundance at every level comes down to a single, relatively simple equation:

Beautiful Money goal + expenses = income intention

This equation might seem completely backward. But the truth is, the equation most people use to manage their money (current income – expenses = save what's left over) is what actually *causes* them to feel like they can't get ahead, are living paycheck to paycheck, or simply don't have enough money. Subtracting our expenses from our income and hoping that we'll have funds left over to save for our future undercuts our dreams. Traditional methods for money management, like budgeting, actually minimize our earning potential. By definition, the amount we earn today is exactly what we have to spend and save. We earn nothing less, and nothing more. We may intend to save what's left over every two weeks, but that's hard to do in real life. Even if we do manage to save some money using traditional strategies, it never seems to be enough.

However, when we approach money management using the Beautiful Money equation, we treat our income as an annual, or even monthly, benchmark that needs to be achieved instead of as a lump sum that just happens to arrive on a biweekly basis. Here's a simple illustration of how the path works. Let's use the example I just shared, my client Allison. Her short-term goal was to purchase a car in cash (without a loan) in six months.

Allison would use the Beautiful Money equation, with six months as her target. She would first set her ideal Beautiful Money income intention for the next six months. Let's say she decided to have twenty thousand dollars saved in six months (fifteen thousand for her car and five thousand to invest). Allison would use this number as her Beautiful Money goal in the equation. She would then calculate her expenses for the upcoming six-month period. (It is important to be very honest with yourself about your expenses. I often recommend having a professional help you calculate this number because we tend to underestimate expenses and even magically forget to include a few.) Let's say Allison calculated her expenses to be three thousand dollars a month, which would work out to be eighteen thousand dollars for the six-month period.

When we plug those numbers into the Beautiful Money equation (see below), it's easy to see how much Allison needs to earn over the next six months to achieve her goal.

Beautiful Money goal + expenses = income intention

So her goal of $20,000 saved (for her car and savings) plus $18,000 expenses (to live and pay bills for the next six months) equals $38,000 total income needed. Divide that by six months, and it equals $6,333 per month (we can say $6,400 to cover our bases and give Allison a little wiggle room).

Keep in mind that Allison might not currently make $6,400 each and every month. In fact, I know she didn't! But because Allison *knows* how much she needs to earn to make her dreams a reality, she's created clarity. And being clear about what we want and how to get there provides a very powerful incentive to act with excellence to make this dream a reality.

Even more important, that clarity provides positive momentum toward all the dates and goals we set for ourselves. As Allison breaks her numbers down more, she realizes she needs to earn sixteen hundred dollars a week (two hundred more per week than she currently does). She is now totally aware of her income intention and can work on a plan to make this happen and create an extra two hundred dollars per week.

Can you see how working forward instead of backward (waiting to see what's left to save) is healthier, more powerful, and more fun? This is visionary leadership in action! You first have to get laser focused on your intended income. Once this is calculated, you can powerfully move toward getting your emotions and your body in alignment with this meaningful prosperity number. When you include your expenses and your savings goals in your final income goal, you work from the driver's seat instead of the passenger seat, and you affirm your intention of creating Beautiful Money.

As you'll see next week, the Beautiful Money equation can be used for any money goal. Whether it's increasing your overall net worth, setting your annual income goal, financing your dream house or business, creating a college savings fund for your children, or achieving financial freedom, the equation remains the same.

Simply figure out when you want to achieve your goal—months, years, maybe even decades for retirement—and then make a rough estimate of how much money that particular goal requires. Keep in mind that it's always best to overestimate, not underestimate. Add in what you expect your expenses to be over that period of time, and—voilà!—you have the amount of money you need to earn to make all your goals and dreams a reality.

I encourage you to use this equation several times for several dates. I like to calculate multiple income intentions, so I know my targets and have key dates. These dates and numbers help create a holistic plan. They also help with long-term and short-term planning. It's amazing to see the momentum created when you are clear and concise with your money.

Use the Beautiful Money equation as often as you wish and at least annually. Using it to figure your three-, five-, and ten-year goals is also amazing! I like to have monthly, quarterly, and annual income intentions. I do like simplicity, so when I first started using the equation, I did it once a year for my annual income intention. I started off by using this equation every December to plan for the upcoming year. I would take a few hours at a coffee shop to set my intentions and goals for the following year, and I would use this formula to help calculate my income target. There is no better feeling than starting your year with complete clarity and a deep commitment to lead from a place of creation and expansion. When you have clarity and know your numbers, you can put the right people and the right plan in place to make it happen.

Beautiful Money Tip

*C*ALCULATING YOUR EXPENSES over long periods of time can be tricky. As a general rule, it's smart to add 10 or 15 percent to current expenses to adjust for factors that are out of your control, like cost of living, taxes, and inflation. However, if you are trying to calculate expenses over years or decades, I suggest consulting an accountant or financial adviser to determine a more exact figure for your specific lifestyle and goals.

Attaching a financial figure to each of the goals and dates we set earlier in this week creates an amazing amount of clarity and motivation, both consciously and subconsciously. We are no longer in the passenger seat in our lives, hoping our paychecks are enough.

Instead, we are in the driver's seat, making our own decisions about how much money we need and, more important, *why* that money matters in our lives. Remember, the intention behind our actions is what truly matters most.

Now that you've calculated exactly how much money it will take for you to reach your freedom dates, you may be wondering how to increase your income to make those numbers materialize. The key is to prioritize profits, which is what we'll discuss in step two.

STEP TWO: PRIORITIZE PROFITS

So now that you know exactly how much money you will need to reach your freedom dates, how can you increase your income to meet those goals (like Allison had to)? As a leader, mentor, and coach, I'm asked a lot of questions about creating holistic wealth, but what people ask most often by far is, "How do I make more money?"

My answer is simple, and it's always the same:

"How much of your time at work is focused on revenue-generating activities?"

This may seem puzzling, but the answer to both questions can usually be found in *your* answer to the latter. Let me explain.

THE 80/20 RULE

The reason most of us have been unable to create wealth in the past is that we spend 80 percent of our time on activities that have zero value and produce zero results, financially or otherwise. When I teach the Beautiful Money course, I ask my students to quickly calculate how much time they spend on revenue-generating activities—and it's usually less than an hour a day! We have a tendency, in both our work and our personal lives, to get caught up in trivial and busy activities that can keep us broke.

We can often instantly increase our income by reducing or eliminating time spent on activities that don't move us forward in our lives. I typically have my clients reduce television time or set aside a specific slot of time on a Sunday when they have permission to fully embrace any trivial activity they want without feeling guilty or nonproductive.

The key to generating more money than ever before is to concentrate on the well-known but rarely practiced 80/20 rule: the *minority* of our efforts creates the *majority* of results. What this means in plain English is that usually there are only a few tasks in our day that actually make us money, provide fulfillment, or add value to our lives. If we just focused on these two or three tasks, we could likely get our work done in a third of the time and have loads more time to enjoy life and take care of ourselves and our family. In an overstimulated world, it takes focus and discipline to follow this rule on a daily basis. Chaos and disorder wants to creep into our lives and mess with us and our profits. Your role is to consistently cleanse your life of chaos and disorder, and to keep focused on the few activities that really matter.

The key to doing less and earning more is figuring out which activities actually create the biggest return—financially, emotionally, and spiritually. Actually doing this is transformational. Many people might claim to know this but haven't clearly identified on paper what these activities are. This is not a good thing. It results in leaving one's days to chance and madly rushing through life thinking there is never enough time.

In my own work with clients, there tend to be only a few activities that truly create returns. Consider your to-do list for today or this week. What three things are going to generate revenue and produce the greatest returns? What would happen if you just concentrated on those three things?

Practicing the 80/20 rule is hard to do simply because most of us are addicted to doing more and more. We feel accomplished when we complete trivial tasks like answering e-mails or keeping up on social media, because they're easier than the big stuff. But when we consider that these efforts don't actually produce results, it's easy to see that we're wasting our time. I actually stopped creating to-do lists several years ago. Instead, I begin each week with an action plan that lays out three revenue-generating intentions. I focus my work on those activities, and relegate the less important tasks (like returning voice messages and e-mails) to a few hours every weekend. This might frustrate people who are used to getting a response in an instant, but always remember: This is your only life. Do you want to spend it on the trivial or the transformational?

This shift in mind-set has completely changed my daily routine, allowing me to spend more time doing what's truly important— being with my family, practicing yoga, and attending to the few work activities that generate income. Frankly, this is the answer I give all the people who ask me how I manage to accomplish everything I do. I simply create the space and time in my schedule to complete what needs to get done. As Jim Rohn says in many of his audio programs: "Learn to say no to the good so you can say yes to the great."[18] And by doing so, I've learned to prioritize, prioritize, prioritize—and you can too!

Beautiful Money Tip

*A*S WITH MOST major shifts in behavior and perspective, transitioning to an 80/20 lifestyle can be intimidating and uncomfortable at first. You will likely feel ungrounded and a little anxious when you get started. This is completely normal. Often, my clients worry that doing less will reduce their income or affect their business success. But we need to remember that the universe needs us to let go, to allow it to work on our behalf, in order to truly create the abundance we desire. Creating Beautiful Money happens when you let go, not when you learn more. Knowledge and learning are absolutely important, but the real shift to a harmonious flow of abundance happens when you let go of that something in your life that is holding you back, weighing you down, or no longer serving you. Part of that process is taking a step back and letting the universe steer you in a positive direction.

Whether it's turning off your phone and Wi-Fi so you can get an important task done or prioritizing a project that you've put off, I'd like for you to practice the 80/20 rule this week simply by *not* spending work or business time on activities that don't create a substantial return on

the effort you invest. This may be hard at first, but I promise that you will see a big difference if you trust that the
universe has your back.

As I'm working right now, my cell is turned over so I
don't see texts or e-mails coming in. It takes practice and
discipline to remove distractions from your environment
when you're creating. When you keep the 80/20 philosophy in mind, you will be amused at how many trivial distractions want to steal your attention and energy. Observe
what happens emotionally when you are not triggered to
let yourself become distracted. Can you discipline yourself
enough to not respond to that text right away? Can you
keep yourself off e-mail? Can you turn off the Wi-Fi without
freaking out? How about turning off all notifications?

Figuring out where to concentrate your effort and time can be
difficult, because it's not always superobvious what the three most
important activities are. Some careers and businesses have very
obvious core activities that generate income. Accountants, con-
tractors, and lawyers, for example, need billable hours. When
these professionals work with clients, they are getting paid. Some
careers or businesses have less obvious activities that generate
income. I'll share some exercises later on to help you prioritize,
but for now remember that the 80/20 rule isn't solely about money
or work. It's about freeing up time and effort and mental space for
what you truly value—and putting your core values first, in order
to separate the vital few from the chaotic many that can prevent
us from creating Beautiful Money.

I still find it fascinating that throughout my career my favorite
mentors and leaders never seemed to be rushed or chaotic. Their
desks were always clean and they enjoyed time with family. But
now I know that's because these people use the 80/20 philosophy
to help them flow into greatness!

Beautiful Money Tip

*I*F YOU LOVE meditating, exercising, practicing yoga, taking an evening bath, or just dedicating a period of time each day to check in with yourself and loved ones, these activities can and should be considered part of your 20 percent (your must-dos). Success is an illusion if we value business over family, health, and well-being. When we prioritize our well-being below business activities, we are out of alignment with Beautiful Money. Even though there may be no immediate financial return for taking care of yourself, building up the mental and emotional reserves to do what you do well is just as important—if not more—to creating Beautiful Money as avoiding chaos.

Your first priority should be to ensure your temple of self (your body, mind, and spirit) is in harmonious alignment with well-being, so you can shine your light brightly into the world and allow those around you to see what you're really made of. Your top priority in this lifetime should be to shine your life force as brightly as possible on the world around you. This means putting yourself first and respecting yourself as a whole.

Remember, to create Beautiful Money we need to think and behave differently. The truth is that most people spend 95 percent of their day at work doing all the wrong things. When it comes to efficiency and revenue-generating activities, most of us have never been taught to take the time to recognize what actually makes a difference in our income and success, and to prioritize precisely those activities.

Instead, we worship the false idol of busyness. We believe that if we're not busy every single day, if our schedule isn't completely crammed with doing stuff, then we're not important and we're not achieving success. But in reality the opposite is true. Beautiful Money is about moving in the opposite direction of the herd. Just because everyone else is scrambling, busy, and exhausted doesn't mean you should be. Maybe it's time for a new personal philosophy—the Beautiful Money 80/20 philosophy.

The Beautiful Money
TIME TRACKER

THIS IS ONE of my absolute favorite exercises because it shows, on paper, how much time we spend doing stuff that doesn't matter. In this exercise, you'll track your activity every morning, afternoon, and evening for a week. Keep in mind that the timing doesn't have to be exact.

Your morning might, for example, include a workout before you go to the office, eating breakfast, attending a meeting, and answering e-mails. A typical evening for most people includes activities like commuting, eating dinner with family, watching TV, taking kids to sports or extracurricular activities, or reading a book. Try to be specific, but don't worry about breaking the time down into exact blocks. Including three or four activities for each segment of the day is usually sufficient for the purpose of this exercise.

At the end of the week, count the activities you wrote down. Then take a highlighter, or a pen with different-colored ink, and circle all the activities that create income directly, produce demonstrable results, or are aligned with your core values (for example yoga class, activities with your family, or volunteer work). Next, count the activities that are circled. Divide the number of circled activities by the number of total activities to get a percentage.

For example, let's take a look at a time tracker for my client Samantha.

Beautiful Money
TIME TRACKER

DAY 1

Morning Activities
- Made family breakfast
- Got kids ready for school
- Drove husband, kids, and self to school/work (2 hours)
- Morning staff meeting

Afternoon Activities
- Ate lunch while reading articles online
- Attended all-hands meeting at work; followed up with my team

Evening Activities
- Commuted home
- Made dinner and helped kids with homework
- Watched TV

DAY 2

Morning Activities
- Got up early to work out
- Commuted to work (1 hour)
- Morning staff meeting

Afternoon Activities
- Did a volunteer event with staff (in lieu of working half the day)

Evening Activities
- Commuted home
- Cooked dinner for kids; coordinated with babysitter
- Spent evening out with husband (dinner and drinks)

DAY 3

Morning Activities
- Made family breakfast
- Got kids ready for school
- Drove husband, kids, and self to school/work (2 hours)
- Morning staff meeting

Afternoon Activities
- Went to lunch with a friend
- Checked e-mails
- Attended a project status meeting with my team

Evening Activities
- Commuted home
- Made dinner and helped kids with homework

DAY 4

Morning Activities
- Got up early to work out
- Commuted to work (1 hour)
- Morning staff meeting

Afternoon Activities
- Went to financial planning meeting
- Spoke to HR about hiring and firing staff

Evening Activities
- Commuted home (1 hour)
- Had my parents over for dinner with the kids

DAY 5

Morning Activities
- Made family breakfast
- Got kids ready for school
- Drove husband, kids, and self to school/work (2 hours)
- Morning staff meeting

Afternoon Activities
- Ate lunch while reading articles online

Evening Activities
- Went to a yoga class
- Made dinner for myself and husband
- Watched TV

She wrote down forty total activities but only high-lighted fifteen, so 15 ÷ 40 = .375 (or 37.5 percent). That means only roughly a third of her week generated any benefit. You may be surprised to hear that Samantha's results are better than most.

Typically, when my clients perform this exercise, less than 10 percent of their time ends up being circled or highlighted. This is important because when our schedule is filled with doing things we don't like (or that cause stress or tension), tasks that don't matter, or activities that don't match our core values or our goals, we simply cannot create Beautiful Money.

Creating Beautiful Money is not about accomplishing our to-do lists or valuing ourselves by how many items are on those lists. Instead, it's about aligning our time with what makes us happy, healthy, and prosperous. The time-tracker exercise helps us clarify what activities create value and which do not, so that we can better align our time and create more Beautiful space for greatness. Less is always more. Both the 80/20 rule and the time-tracker exercise provide the evidence that we need to reconsider how we spend our time. Shouldn't we be calculating our personal return on the investment of our time and energy? We often have to crunch this equation at work, but we rarely do it for our life. What's even more absurd is that although many people might claim to earn a six-figure salary, if they calculate their personal return on investment, they may be shocked at what they really earn. If they are burning the midnight oil for work, working weekends, and sacrificing their health, how much does their salary really equate to hourly? They might be in for a scary surprise.

If you are shocked by your time-tracker results, you're not alone. When I was in my twenties, I examined my schedule and realized that I spent most of my time at a day job, traveling like a crazy person to live paycheck to paycheck, with zero personal time. The only activity I did outside work was train for marathons. I hadn't created the time tracker yet, but if I had, I bet my result would have been less than 5 percent.

Not spending time on what we truly value in life is a big problem, to be sure, but it becomes a massive problem when we don't do anything about it. We must decide to change the way we spend our time and what activities we prioritize. Once we do that, we move ourselves to the driver's seat when it comes to creating wealth.

THE WEALTH DISCONNECT

IT CAN BE shocking to realize that we're spending our life doing things we don't like, worrying about things that aren't important, or imploding from stress—just by being too busy! I call this the "wealth disconnect."

- People don't spend enough time identifying the few essentials that will create more success and wealth
- People spend too much time working harder trying to manage chaos
- People spend more money, are less effective, and are more likely to burn out when their schedules are jammed
- People spend most of their time worrying about or feeling afraid of events and situations that will likely never happen

- ◆ People let others' opinions influence their decisions
- ◆ People are starved of personal and financial leverage by being attached to their work and jobs 24-7

Does this resonate? It did for me. The truth is that our societal norms—which value long nights at the office, being attached to e-mail 24-7, and making work our first priority— are exactly the opposite of what creates harmonious and sustainable wealth. That's why I call it a "disconnect."

By reorganizing our schedule and prioritizing the work that actually creates returns, we can generate more income, create better results, *and* no longer waste our energy and time on tasks that don't matter.

When we look at our time-tracker results, it's easy to see the wasted activities—watching TV, checking social media, doing nonproductive work, answering e-mails, coordinating meetings, avoiding work by watching YouTube videos . . . I would guess that for the average person, there are at least ten hours of nonaligned, nonproductive, non-revenue-generating time in any given week. I am of course an advocate of making time for hobbies and passions (and I do love movies), but when it becomes a daily norm to check out at night in front of the television, this is where the time tracker can be helpful to identify patterns that may be creating a wealth disconnect.

That said, we can practice being less distracted by external forces like chaos and busywork by establishing better habits. This is yet another example of saying no to the good to make room for the great. By eliminating a task that is good but not essential— like responding to e-mails or texts quickly—we create time to work on what creates income. That doesn't mean we won't answer our e-mails (we'll make time for that when the revenue-generating activities are completed), but we will open up space in our schedule for activities that both generate income and reflect our core values. By not being tied to our e-mail accounts, we may find that we have more time for our families and ourselves.

When I realized how much time I was wasting answering e-mails, I was shocked. I realized I was a gofer for technology. I have found that scheduling specific times to check e-mails and texts helps me create the discipline I need to truly prioritize my time.

After doing the time tracker, I identified three elements of my business that actually generated income and I focused on doing them only from Monday to Friday. I threw out my to-do list because I didn't need it anymore. If an activity wasn't one of those three things, I pushed it to the weekend. And as a result, my income grew every month. I find that, as a rule of thumb, most of us have only three activities in our business that truly generate revenue—and that's what we should spend our time on if we intend to prioritize profits.

THE WEEKLY WEALTH AND WELL-BEING PLAN

I AM A goal-setting superfan. I have always set goals and have made it an annual and a weekly practice to write them down. Not only does this habit help you get superclear about what you deeply desire, but it also helps you to avoid or eliminate trivial or nonaligned activities that steal your energy and your time.

In order to eliminate busywork and align our time and effort with what truly matters, we need to replace our daily to-do lists with a weekly action plan (I call this my "weekly wealth and well-being plan"): three inspiring and juicy goals that will bring us the greatest personal and professional return this week.

Each week (I like to complete this on Sunday evening), we should select three exciting and inspiring goals that we intend to achieve. Remember that the Beautiful Money philosophy is to write down these three goals, without attachment. We should put our heart, soul, and excellence into achieving these goals, but if we don't quite complete everything, we shouldn't be hard on ourselves or make a judgment.

How do you emotionally handle yourself at the end of the week if these goals aren't complete? Just give yourself an extension! How simple is that? There's no need to judge yourself, be hard on yourself, or treat yourself unkindly! Pat yourself on the back if you gave the week your all and follow this up with being gentle and kind with yourself. Simply write these goals down again the following week.

Your weekly wealth and well-being plan is your opportunity to become the architect of your life. On a weekly basis, you can design your life any way you choose and have at your fingertips the opportunity to become clearer and more focused as you go. It doesn't matter where you begin!

I often get asked how to know what three goals are worthy of making the weekly wealth and well-being plan. I like to suggest that they are the ones that might move you out of your comfort zone and create a few butterflies in your stomach but not halt you in your tracks with nausea.

It should be somewhere between the comfort zone (you could do it with your eyes closed) and cliff jumping, in other words, depending on your personality and your experience with goal setting. It is important to consider how deeply you believe in yourself. If you are working on developing a strong sense of confidence and self, start with three weekly goals you know you can achieve but that will hold you accountable to working with excellence. "Baby steps" is always my recommendation when we're just starting on our Beautiful Money journey.

Generating wealth and creating Beautiful Money is a daily practice. When I work with individual clients, it can be easy for me to see why they aren't achieving their next level of financial greatness. Most of the time, it's because their daily habits and activities work in opposition to their desired goals. The most obvious is someone who wants to save more but continually uses shopping to release emotional tension, or someone who claims to value health but eats fast food or drinks alcohol several times a week.

The fact is, we are all distractible and can fall victim to addictive habits when life gets crazy and when we forget to prioritize ourselves. Before I became a mom, I was disciplined, developed great habits, and experienced incredible flow. I had worked on, and healed, my addictions to spending, carbs, sugar, and emotional eating.

But after my kids arrived? Forget about it! I felt like I'd regressed to kindergarten. I rarely made time to eat (my husband told people I lived off air), had difficulty staying grounded, and lost every second of my personal time. As I mentioned before, I am a sensitive soul and personal time is my saving grace. It helps me digest and process, and it's critical to keeping me grounded. But with three kids under the age of three, I had zero personal time. I am a work in progress and am always relearning boundaries and self-care routines as a mom and a wiser entrepreneur. I've since learned how to adapt my schedule to be an awesome parent and practice what I preach in terms of habits, but this is definitely still an area where I can continue to improve. And so can you.

Want to know my greatest secret? You have to learn not to care so much about what people think of you. I was watching an episode of *The Good Wife* (yes, when I'm off duty I'm off duty) and the character Alicia shared that failure was her greatest blessing. The exhaustion and emotional toll associated with it resulted in her caring less. Although the spin was not a positive one, I could relate to this so much in my own life.

If you are stubbornly holding on to habits and ways that are not serving you, the universe will eventually crush you into fine wine. Disappointing people and learning to care less what other people thought of me were two areas where I had to be crushed into a fine Malbec. But it was worth it.

In my experience, two categories of habits make us healthy, wealthy, and wise: Beautiful Money (lifestyle) habits and wealth (financial) habits. Let's examine the way we live first.

Beautiful Money Habits

- ◆ I wake up early feeling refreshed and inspired.
- ◆ I have clear and focused goals.
- ◆ I surround myself with positive energy and people.
- ◆ I limit negativity from TV, news, and people.
- ◆ I practice grounding activities (walks, yoga, meditation, being outdoors).
- ◆ I review my spending, cash flow, and income regularly.
- ◆ I nourish my body with water, supplements, and healthy, whole foods.

- I practice being ahead of schedule to avoid feeling rushed.
- I say no when it's required and avoid overcommitting.
- I practice being authentic and speaking my truth over people-pleasing.
- I strive to underpromise and overdeliver (big one!).
- I ask for help.
- I set clear boundaries.
- I schedule space in my calendar.
- I align my activities with my goals and values (80/20 rule).
- I do things with efficiency and excellence.
- I cleanse my environment daily of what doesn't serve me.
- I keep my car, office, bedroom, and home clean and clear.
- I have a daily self-care or healing ritual.
- I do fifteen minutes of personal development daily.
- I practice living drama-free.
- I tune in to my emotional state (attachments and addictions).
- I breathe deeply throughout the day and in times of tension.
- I get a good night's sleep.
- I avoid chaos and chaotic situations.
- I let go and release unwanted and unhealthy energy daily.
- I lead by example, with love and light.
- I nourish my soul and spirit daily.
- I treat my time just before I fall asleep and just as I wake up as sacred and precious. These are perfect moments to work with my subconscious to create what I truly desire.

Think about your routine. How many of these habits do you incorporate on a daily basis? Mark those habits with a check. If there are only a few, that's okay. Including as many of the Beautiful Money habits into your lifestyle as is reasonable (without causing stress) will benefit you physically and emotionally.

If you have just begun on the Beautiful Money journey, start small and simple: implement just one new habit. For my wellness clients, the most important first habit I recommend implementing is drinking water throughout the day. Simple is always better.

The key to replacing the habits that have held us back with those that truly create Beautiful Money is to not be hard on yourself, to give yourself permission to not be perfectly aligned each and every day, and to allow yourself to get back on track with better habits over time. It will become easier, I promise. Judging yourself or being hard on yourself will instantly throw you out of alignment with Beautiful Money.

To help get you started, I'm going to share a delicious exercise that allows us to ditch old habits that no longer serve us while simultaneously learning how to incorporate new habits that tweak our lifestyle and our ability to create wealth for the better.

Take out a sheet of paper. Write down any old habits that aren't serving you anymore and that move you away from achieving your freedom dates. Be superhonest, because you don't have to show this to anyone. What habits do you have that you hide from others? What habits wouldn't you want to share with the world? What habits don't feel right in your body? In the past, clients have written down things like "eating junk food" and "stop checking e-mail before bed." Any habits that are not healthy or aligned with where you want to go, and that no longer serve you, should appear on that piece of paper. Next, practice reading what you just wrote on that piece of paper, not as yourself, but as an observer (as if someone else had these habits). This will help you to shift from judging yourself harshly. If a friend came to you in confidence and shared these habits, would you shame her? Then don't shame yourself!

Now destroy that piece of paper. Burn it. Throw it in the ocean. Toss it in the wind. Rip it up. Shred it into a million pieces with scissors. Whatever feels right to you. Breathe. Take a moment to listen to an inspiring song, meditate, or simply sit calmly.

Take out another piece of paper. Write down all the new habits you'd like to incorporate daily. Try to fill up the entire piece of paper. Like you did with your freedom dates, don't worry about how you are going to get there or actually start incorporating these habits. Just write everything down. When you're done, pick a habit or two that really speaks to you, a habit that will help you to feel abundant, aligned, healthy, and true to yourself. Highlight these one or two habits and post your paper somewhere in your home where you will see it often (bathroom mirror, fridge, office, bedroom, etc.). Make a point of doing those things, of making those habits into habits, each and every day for as long as you're reading this book. Remember, don't be hard on yourself if you can't do whatever that new habit is each and every day. If you need accountability, ask a partner or a friend to remind you why you've chosen this habit as a way to start changing your life. (Or you can set a reminder on your phone to practice it daily, whatever works better for you.) Remember, creating Beautiful Money is all about creating momentum and gracefully propelling your life into a higher state of abundance and joy.

Prioritizing what we do in a day and consciously choosing what we want to spend our time and effort on provides the push forward that we need to break out of old habits and generate a new lifestyle of wealth and wisdom. This takes deep commitment and discipline. Remember that disorder constantly wants to creep into your life and mess with you. I'll share some practical methods that provide even more momentum next, in the final step of Week Three. Are you ready for even more greatness?

STEP THREE:
BECOME YOUR OWN BANK

Imagine how freeing and powerful it would feel to never need financial assistance or a loan. Imagine always having the resources and cash to fund whatever you desire. What if people came to you to borrow money, to ask advice on their mortgages, to ask questions about how to create abundance, or to strategize about holistic wealth? This is one of my ultimate goals in life. I want to become my own bank. This idea may not appeal to you, but just contemplate the possibility of never needing to ask anyone else for money or financial advice again.

This final step of Week Three will help you adapt the concept of becoming your own bank to your own needs. You are going to learn the basics of managing your own finances, starting today. How far you want to take these principles and how excited you become about money management is up to you. (Personally, I get really hyper and pumped when I talk about this. I become full of energy and enthusiasm.) No matter where you are in terms of your financial health, the advice and strategies in this step will help you become more abundant and ready to create Beautiful Money.

Beautiful Money Tip

EVERYONE WHO COMES to Beautiful Money is in a different place financially. Wherever you are in this moment is a great place to start, because the path to Beautiful Money can begin anywhere.

The fact of the matter is, everyone who comes to Beautiful Money seeks a harmonious flow of wealth and well-being. That's why people feel driven to take my course or buy this book. We tend to hoard money, save too little, or spend every dime we have. It's okay to need help managing money; at some point almost everyone does. Our first step in becoming our own bank and learning how to manage our money in a beautiful, prosperous way is to explore the behaviors that have held us back from the next level of holistic wealth—until now.

WHAT'S YOUR PATTERN?

Spend more than you earn

Spend everything you earn

Save more than you spend

Save everything (hoard money because you are afraid to spend because you fear not having enough)

It's important to recognize what you've done with your money up until this point. Do you feel like you're always catching up because you spend too much? Or are you zeroing out your accounts week after week because you don't know what to do with anything that's left over? (That was what I did in my twenties!) Or are you in a fearful position, afraid to spend a dime lest the bottom drop out? Are you afraid that you will never have enough money? Are you afraid one day you're going to lose all your money? Are you clueless as to where all your money goes?

Now isn't the time to judge or be hard on yourself for the pattern you identify most with. What is important, though, is to be honest with yourself, as acknowledging your pattern will likely help you have a money aha moment. Also, if you are in a relationship, your partner's saving and spending pattern can be important to consider, since conflicting patterns create—you guessed it—conflict.

Beautiful Money Tip

*I*F YOU'RE CURRENTLY in a relationship, it is, I believe, extremely helpful (and an accelerant to the creation of Beautiful Money) for both of you to honestly identify your money pattern to date and write out any fears you have around money.

Committing to having open discussions about money can also be very helpful. If you're a money hoarder and your partner is a mad spender, you likely have relationship issues around money.

Regardless of where you are, acknowledge the behaviors and habits that have brought you here, and renew your commitment to change. Remember, all the hard work you've done thus far has set you on the path to success with the exercises in this week and throughout the rest of the book. What we're doing now will help you use simple actions to create great transformation and a healthier, more prosperous existence.

CREATE BEAUTIFUL WEALTH HABITS

Developing good wealth habits is important for creating harmonious wealth and wellness, as well as for continuing to live in the flow of Beautiful Money. Some of the habits I've listed on the next two pages sound so simple. But when we're busy, these practices can suddenly seem less important. Like adopting Beautiful Money habits, these wealth habits should be incorporated into our lives one at a time, to reduce the chance of overwhelm and stress. It's totally fine—even best—to begin with baby steps toward that big Beautiful Money world.

- I spend less than I earn
- I save more than I need to (I am a happy and healthy saver)
- I recognize that cash flow (and a reserve fund) is queen
- I review my spending weekly
- I don't spend to release emotional energy
- I have weekly, quarterly, and annual income goals
- I have a wealth team in place
- I am a money and wealth student always
- I give myself permission to learn from my mistakes
- I prioritize my spending based on core values
- I respect the energy of money
- I automate investing and saving activities
- I have vehicles and planning in place to increase cash flow
- I focus on money results and not excuses
- I review my finances and statements regularly
- I have tax strategies in place
- I surround myself with people who raise me up
- I review and reduce banking fees on a regular basis
- I automate investing and saving activities
- I save throughout the year for taxes
- I pay bills as soon as they come in
- I set daily priorities that are aligned with Beautiful Money
- I limit the number of credit cards I have (personally, I used to have only a single credit card, but when I became a mom and began to travel internationally I decided to get a second one)
- I stay free and clear of bad debt

- I prioritize my spending based on my core values
- I spend on my needs before my wants
- I have a system for tracking my spending
- I focus on creating wealth
- I limit credit card spending and manage it well
- I have my estate and financial affairs in order (always)

We'll talk more about how these wealth habits relate to managing our money, but before we get there I'd like to point out a few wealth habits that I think are important enough to be a part of everyone's daily routine.

I spend less than I earn.

Small purchases, like digital subscriptions, add up quickly. Are you spending money on items that you don't need? Examining your bank statements monthly, or even weekly, can help you see where you are spending money unnecessarily. I have also found that reviewing your automatic payments on a regular basis is important, to make sure these are still aligned with your goals.

For entrepreneurs, tools for contact management, webinars, online bookkeeping, e-mail management (and on and on) can add up, and we can forget to cancel ones we rarely use or no longer need. Make a list of all your automatic monthly payments and review them often.

I automate investing and savings activities.

Seriously, this is the easiest habit to begin—you just set it and forget it. We'll talk more about how much money you should automatically save or invest in the next section, but this is an easy habit to incorporate and one that will make your life so much easier. I have an automatic withdrawal every week from my checking account that goes into a no-fee savings account. When that savings account reaches a certain figure, I give it to my financial professional to invest. Last year, a client realized that she never put money into her IRA because she manually had to transfer the funds. She set up an automatic transfer each month from her savings account and told me, "Leanne, it was like magic. I never even noticed that the money was gone." I also automate my savings to go toward taxes and my investments with my financial adviser. Everything is automated in my world. If it were left up to me, my old habit of spending everything I earn would likely take over and leave nothing left to save.

I recognize that cash flow (a reserve fund) is queen.

In 2015 my husband, Ric, and I had three situations in which we would have been in serious financial trouble if we hadn't had a reserve fund and a fabulous passive income stream in the wellness industry to tap into for unexpected expenses. I am grateful every day. Although I don't live from a place of fear, things can happen that you don't expect. For us, that included a renovation that turned messy and financially onerous. Most financial professionals advise building a fund that will cover six to twelve months of your expenses, and I think that's a great idea. If you don't already have this, make having a substantial reserve fund one of your financial goals this year. (Set an abundance date for it!) In my experience, one of the key reasons (aside from not saving) we end up in a financial mess is not having a healthy cash flow. When we are always tight for cash, we can't help but feel stressed, weighted down, and full of tension. When we're worried about paying our bills, we don't sleep well because we're always wondering what's coming in next week and next month. We have trouble being fully present because of our "missing" money.

For women especially, lacking cash flow can move you out of your feminine flow and into a more masculine energy state. This is because you're tense, angry, frustrated, and likely chasing money. There's nothing more divine than building a healthy cash flow reserve so you can sleep wealthy and healthy. When you aren't stressed about cash flow, you can soften into your beautiful feminine flow and experience life feeling kind, graceful, abundant, and soft. This is why in my opinion cash flow is queen.

I review my spending weekly.

This is so simple, but not that many of us do it. At the beginning of your Beautiful Money journey, I recommend that you try to live entirely on cash for a week. The results will blow your mind and put in perspective the calculations you're about to make in the next section.

A great way to track your spending on a regular basis is to ask for, and keep, all receipts for every transaction you make. At the end of the day or the week, organize the receipts into two categories: one for personal expenses and one for business. (You can also divide receipts into needs and wants.) To track how you are spending over time, create a simple ledger in which you enter the totals every night or every week. This is an easy way to see how much you spend, where you can make cuts, and how to allocate money overall. I also like to reserve an hour or two on Fridays to get organized, review my finances, file my receipts, and pay any outstanding bills. It makes me feel clean, clear, and ready with open arms for more Beautiful Money.

I don't spend to release emotional energy.

Shopping can be an emotional release and a way to avoid your own feelings. Dairy Queen Blizzards and shopping were two of my emotional outlets. Like being dependent on alcohol or eating junk food, any addiction can show us where we need to change and where we're not dealing with something emotionally. When I realized that the highlight of my day was a

Dairy Queen Blizzard and a trip to my favorite boutique, I knew something was seriously wrong. It took time and patience, but I finally committed to a life detox and a spending freeze. For a year, I bought almost nothing: no clothes, shoes, furniture, knickknacks—pretty much nothing. It was challenging at first (especially when I was in a funk because it was the time when I would typically go shopping) but became exhilarating. I would spend money only on life expenses and wellness activities (yoga, workshops, and massages). That year was one of the most freeing and healthy years of my life. It helped me realize how much I had been stuffing down my feelings—and it put me on the road to Beautiful Money.

These are just a few of the habits that can help you build wealth. I started by focusing on the ones that were meaningful to me. By incorporating these new habits into your daily life one at a time, you will slowly start to change your patterns around money and build a more healthy relationship with your own finances, thereby opening the door to holistic wealth.

MY SLEEP-WEALTHY BUDGET

It sounds simple, but creating a high-level budget and automating savings is one of the easiest and most effective steps you can take to move toward abundance and financial freedom, starting today.

Typically I recommend:

Living and Necessities: 50 Percent

Expect that a week's income will cover half of your necessary living expenses. This would include your mortgage or rent, groceries, and utilities. Some books and advisers will recommend allocating 75 percent, but I think if we're able to keep our necessary expenses at 50 percent of our income, then we are better able to deal with the unexpected and to live below our means in general. The one exception to this is if you live and work in an urban area where the cost of living is abnormally high; in that case it's possible your costs for basic necessities and living expenses (like rent and groceries) may rise to 60 or even 70 percent. Remember that you can't sleep wealthy and healthy if you feel like barfing every day because there's too much month at the end of the money.

Beautiful Money
Budget for Wealth

Living & Necessities

50%

Investing & Savings

25%

Lifestyle

25%

Investing and Savings: 25 Percent

This figure might be higher than what you're used to, but it covers *all* savings and investment vehicles. Any retirement account contributions that are made through your employer, like a 401(k) or an IRA, would factor in. This 25 percent also includes the following accounts:

Abundant cash flow account
   Otherwise known as an emergency fund (although I wouldn't ever call it that), this is where you should keep cash

equal to a few months' worth of expenses in case of unexpected gaps in income or periods when you may require greater cash flow. Last year our abundant cash flow account came in handy when we suddenly needed a large sum. Having this account allowed us to avoid taking out a bank loan. Having this account will help you sleep better at night, I promise. If you don't have one currently, aim to get the equivalent of at least six months' worth of expenses saved within the next year. If you have been working on building up a reserve fund already, prioritize having the equivalent of your annual salary, just in case. If you don't currently have an abundant cash flow account, open one today!

Automated tax savings account

Depending on whether you are in business for yourself or work for a company, you may need more money in this account. For entrepreneurs who pay taxes on a quarterly basis out of pocket, it's pretty easy to determine how much money needs to be deposited in this account on a weekly or monthly basis. But if you are at a job that takes your taxes out of your paycheck, adding a small sum to this account on a monthly basis can be handy in case you end up generating extra income or your family's tax situation changes.

Automated wealth account

This account is essentially a stopover for funds you want to invest. Make sure that 5 percent of your income is transferred to this account every month. If possible, automate this account so that when it is over a certain amount (say, one thousand or five thousand dollars) that money is directly invested into an asset within your greater portfolio. This will make investing easy and hassle-free. You can also have your financial adviser set this up for you so you don't even have to think; your money just flows into wealth. I am also a fan of leveraging different life insurance plans for "tax smart" wealth creation.

If you would like to investigate this strategy further, speak to an insurance agent, accountant, or specialist in your vicinity. There are fabulous ways to leverage insurance plans to reduce your tax liability and help you grow your net worth. I used to have a negative view of life insurance policies, but after learning more and becoming a mom, I have come to love and leverage these policies. From a tax perspective, it's a smart idea to have a conversation with a well-respected and reputable life insurance agent. I automate a healthy portion of my monthly earnings into several "par" or "whole life" insurance plans. I will speak more about legacy later, but creating your family legacy should always be considered in your day-to-day calculations. Making decisions today that positively impact yourself and your family long term is key.

Lifestyle: 25 Percent

Your "lifestyle cash" might be spent on travel, clothes, dining—anything. For Beautiful Money creation, you will want to link this spending with activities that align with your core values. What I like to do with this account is to make sure I spend any extra money on what I love first—yoga classes, fitness, travel, or a personal-growth seminar—and then use what's left over as play investing money. Maybe my honey and I will buy some land in an underdeveloped area where real estate values are uncertain, for example, or invest in a new venture that seems promising.

If you're not investing or saving very much now, I suggest you minimize lifestyle spending to 10 percent. Before I decided to change my relationship with money, I always struggled to save. One of the ways I shifted my pattern was to totally freeze any discretionary spending for one year. This may sound difficult, if not impossible, but it will help you build fabulous discipline in your life. I allowed myself to spend money on travel, fitness, yoga, and healthy food. If it wasn't in those categories, it wasn't important to me. That taught me to practice mindfulness about spending my hard-earned money on stuff that didn't matter. And I didn't miss what I would have bought before, so the exercise was totally worth it.

Beautiful Money Tip

*I*F UNNECESSARY OR unconscious spending is an issue for you, I recommend setting a weekly limit for gratuitous purchases (i.e., wants, not needs). The limit could be as low as ten dollars or as high as a hundred dollars based on your goals. Remove that amount of money from an ATM at the beginning of the week. You can spend it on anything you want, but that's all you can spend. Trust me, you will be much more aware of how, where, and when you spend than ever before. You will likely be shocked at the amount of money you hemorrhage on trivial things that don't serve you or make you happy.

Automating your finances sounds supereasy, and it is. But the results are amazing; you won't believe how fast your savings and accounts grow if you don't have to think about moving the money around. And since you're not actually taking action, it's easier to challenge your established patterns and shift your focus to what you're working toward, not what you're working against. If you don't yet have a family but are planning on having one, don't do what most people do and wait until your seventh month of pregnancy to start getting your financial life in order! Start saving today. (The same goes for weddings or anything else you know you are going to do in the future.)

CREATING HOLISTIC WEALTH

Wealth creation is about having healthy money assets (especially passive income), leverage, cash flow, and tax strategies.

Beautiful Money streams are incredibly important because these are our wealth builders and money generators. It's important to evaluate whatever income streams you currently have, as well as what streams might be appropriate to incorporate into your lifestyle. If you are an employee, your salary is likely your primary money vehicle (and that's great), but consider adding one of the streams outside of salaried or hourly income to your wealth plan. Although salaried income is fabulous and just might fund your lifestyle, it lacks leverage. If you can't work, don't like your work, or get laid off, you are in a serious financial mess. It's difficult to become your own bank if your sole source of income is generated from a salary or hourly wage. It's important to build your wealth holistically and consider generating money in a variety of ways so you are never caught in a money trap.

Here are five Beautiful Money streams for you to review:

- Passive income: This often results from solidifying a residual income stream. It is when you have money that flows in because of work you've previously done, not work you're still committed to doing. This is true "sleep wealthy" income. With this type of income, you are paid multiple times for work you do once. You may hear this called "royalty" income. This is my favorite type.
- Big assets: This includes real estate, any other significant property, etc. (This is my husband's favorite financial vehicle.)
- Cash: This would include your salary, hourly income, and other liquid assets. Remember that cash flow is queen, but we can fall victim to chasing money or burning out if we aren't careful with this stream option.

- Investments: These include retirement savings, 401(k) accounts, IRAs, whole life or par insurance plans, stocks, bonds, mutual funds, etc.
- Other: Essentially anything else that could provide money if sold or liquidated, like cars, jewelry, antiques, collectibles, etc.

To properly evaluate all your income streams, write down what you currently have and what goals you'd like to achieve for that stream. For instance, I have a goal of putting aside cash because I want my family to have a solid, liquid reserve fund that is available quickly. In the past, I have too heavily invested in assets that couldn't quickly be liquidated (like real estate), so cash flow is my new queen. There may be streams you want to take advantage of, like passive income, which you haven't yet. Those income streams should also be included in this exercise. It's important to remember that not every income stream will be for everyone, so if you're not interested in creating passive income or building up a broad real estate portfolio, it's fine to ignore that category or stream. The core message I want you to take away is that we need more than one income stream to create holistic wealth.

Beautiful Money Tip

Sleep wealthy with passive (residual or royalty) income

The reason most people never get ahead and live from paycheck to paycheck is because they rely on linear income. A good way to think of linear income is that you put in hours and get paid for those hours once. Residual income is different in that it arrives day after day, week after week, year after year, whether you're awake or asleep. There's a limit to the amount of linear income you can create, since there are only twenty-four hours in a day.

Residual income can be earned through direct selling (one of my favorite Beautiful Money streams), royalties, rental or vacation properties (another favorite), investments, and through many online business models. At some point, you'll need a source of residual income — especially given how crazy and unstable an environment the world of corporate jobs and linear income (like salaries) has become. Online business owners also have ways to generate royalty income from vehicles such as membership sites and affiliate programs.

If we start building residual income streams early in life, we'll always have doors open to us — and we won't be dependent on an external entity in order to pay our bills and live comfortably. I was very clear that I wanted to start my residual income stream early in life so if and when I had a family, I'd have all the time in the world to spend with them and would be able to put time with them first. What I have found from experience is that often we wait until we are in a state of panic or emergency to start a residual income stream. It is so much more fun and flowing if you start to build a passive income stream long before you need it.

When I first learned about the different income streams, I didn't have any passive income. I learned a lot about it, then thoroughly researched and chose to partner with my favorite global wellness company. I built my business part time (two to three hours a week) in the beginning and, by partnering with my favorite people, grew it into a global wellness empire. This residual income has funded the purchase of multiple properties, pays all my bills, and funds my dreams. My husband and I are committed to an international lifestyle for our family, and we couldn't have done this without a healthy and aligned residual income stream. A solid residual income stream creates freedom. This is what I was so hungry to create in my life. I longed for a schedule that was spacious and filled with only happy and healthy activities. I longed to take as many vacations in a year as I wanted, on my own terms and whenever I wanted. I desired to sleep healthy and wealthy, and my residual income stream brought this to my life. It also funds my dream projects. My residual income stream has allowed me to hire the best mentors in the world and not compromise my dreams and goals. Some people might prefer real estate or to focus on investing. Whatever you do, I suggest that you follow the advice of one of my mentors, who told me to focus on growing one income stream to about $100,000 residually (per year) before trying to work on another. This strategy isn't for everyone, but it has been an effective and healthy strategy for me, and for many of my clients as well.

Remember, creating Beautiful Money means living in alignment and in flow. This requires clarity, focus, and persistence. Focusing on one (or two) Beautiful Money streams at a time helps us to stay grounded and harmonious.

Beautiful Money Tip

IF YOU ARE currently in a relationship, you might choose to focus on one Beautiful Money stream while your partner focuses on another. This strategy is genius! I started my Beautiful Money journey single, so focusing on a stream outside my day job was healthy for me; it just felt right. Remember, always go with your gut!

Leverage is crucial when it comes to creating wealth. The reason people become trapped in their jobs or burn out is often a lack of leverage. In contrast, having leverage means that you earn money in a passive way—even when you are not "at work." A lack of leverage almost always leads to frustration (and exhaustion) eventually. If we are limited in how much we can earn by the hours each day that we can physically work, we lack leverage. Identifying where you lack leverage both financially (do you need a passive income stream so you can make money while you're sleeping?) and on a personal level (where do you need to ask for help and when and how can you surrender control, the sense that "I can take care of everything"?) can make a huge difference in how much wealth you create. I have found that often our egos keep us broke or barely getting by. Women especially can feel inadequate and subpar if we don't do things ourselves. Heaven forbid we ask others for help! But this do-everything-yourself approach is not healthy and eventually leads to burnout or becoming an angry bird. So don't do it! Figure out when and where you can give up some control to free yourself to do what you are truly meant to do (and create more leverage in the process). Leverage should be your new BFF.

Cash flow is queen, as I've stated throughout this book. We all need liquidity to pay our bills and live on a daily basis. I have found tight cash flow to be the most common situation troubling clients who come to me seeking Beautiful Money.

Imagine sleeping every night knowing you have a hundred thousand or a million dollars sitting pretty, just waiting for you if you ever need it. Wouldn't this help you flow into creativity and exhale with comfort and security? Wouldn't you feel taken care of? Having a healthy dose of accessible cash is good for our bodies and minds.

At a very basic level, if we don't have sufficient cash flow, we have money issues in our tissues. We will never feel safe and secure. Because of that insecurity, we will live out our days chasing money and trying to force success. I have found that a restricted cash flow causes every cell in our body to tense; it affects our mood during the day and our ability to relax and sleep at night. It's possible to have leverage and great assets but not enough cash flow, which is why we need to keep an eye on both asset generation and having ready access to cash.

Tax strategies are also important because we need to properly manage what happens when we make Beautiful Money. As you climb the corporate ladder or expand your entrepreneurial empire, keeping your eye on tax implications is key. If you don't educate yourself and surround yourself with a great tax team, you will likely find yourself in a worse situation than you were in before you started making Beautiful Money. Learn, for example, about capital gains strategies, when to incorporate, and how and why to create a holding company. Tax strategies have become my favorite opportunity for learning. I eat up wisdom from my financial team and cannot get enough of all the different strategies and scenarios. Fears and stress may come up for you when you hear the word "taxes," which is why leveraging wisdom from experts is important. Let experts guide you and advise you about your tax strategy options. As your Beautiful Money flow strengthens, this will become one of the most important areas for you to stay attentive to. Paying taxes is important and healthy, but overpaying taxes isn't part of the Beautiful Money program. I was overpaying for years before I learned more effective strategies. If you don't already have a team in place, ask around for two or three accountant referrals and set up a meeting with each. Always interview a few accountants before selecting yours. Experience is important, but having a healthy personality fit is just as essential.

BUILD A BEAUTIFUL MONEY TEAM

Regardless of how much money you currently have, I always recommend creating your very own Beautiful Money team. You might need only one or two experts on your side in the beginning (an accountant and a financial adviser), but leveraging professionals will help you stay organized and efficient as you build your empire. Whether you are at the beginning of your Beautiful Money journey and want a clear status update of where you are at, or simply want help managing your money long term, building a solid team of professionals is beneficial.

It's important that anyone you hire be a good fit on both a personal and a professional level. Don't just pick the first person you find. Interview everyone, whether it's a certified financial planner or a lawyer to handle your estate. Friends and family you admire, as well as mentors, can be great sources for referrals. Make sure that whomever you consider hiring is a good fit for you as an individual or for your family as a whole. Even if you get a great referral, *always* do your own homework to ensure the referral is a great fit for you. I learned this the hard way. I get referrals on a weekly basis and used to trust the person who sent me the referral. After two key and costly learning opportunities, I realized that even if I get a referral, it's up to me to do my own due diligence.

For example, if you work in the corporate world, you might want a financial adviser who works mainly with individuals who work for companies. If you are in business for yourself, it's important to have an accountant who understands and has experience with your industry, the expenses related to it, and the tax strategies specific to it. If you aren't the greatest at organizing your receipts or at the day-to-day management of your money, a bookkeeper may be well worth the cost.

For your part, be clear on your goals before reaching out to anyone. When we know what we want and need to do to build holistic wealth, we have clarity and can share that vision with whomever we hire. If a member of your team is no longer the greatest fit, let go. Remember, it's your money and your wealth that these people are in charge of. As a rule of thumb, I like to ask any referrals I get two questions:

1. Can you help me with my specific goal of

_____ ?

2. Do you have specific experience with

_____ ?

The more specific your questions are, the greater clarity you will gain as to whether the referral is a good fit for you and your situation.

There are many paths to achieving abundance, but building leverage, creating cash flow, using tax strategies, and capitalizing on all possible Beautiful Money streams are constructive ways to create and sustain the positive momentum that leads to your next level of greatness—designing your destination, which is the topic of Week Four.

WEEK FOUR

WEEK FOUR

Design Your Destination

I HAVE TO ADMIT, this last week is my favorite!

We will use the clarity, space, and focus you've created over the past three weeks to design a new lifestyle that will not only increase your income but also augment your sense of self-worth and abundance. This is where our creative juices and energy transform our vision into tangible results.

In step one, I will teach you how to make a clear, conscious decision that solidifies your commitment to change and shows you how to map out your intention to grow your net worth in the future (specifically, over the next five years). We'll put our intentions into action by setting three amazing, juicy, and audacious goals that will create the momentum for you to bring into being what you truly desire from life.

In step two, I'll share my secrets on how to become a money magnet, attracting wealth everywhere you go, and how to avoid becoming a money monster, someone who is consumed by the idea and action of generating money just to be wealthy, which is exactly the opposite of Beautiful Money. We'll also tackle how to handle the haters you may encounter when you begin to reap the rewards of all the changes you've made while experiencing this program and traveling the path to holistic wealth.

And, finally, in step three I will explain how the four L's—leadership, leverage, legacy, and love—factor into creating Beautiful Money on a daily basis and help you maintain momentum so all the change, clarity, and space you've created in the past three weeks will keep taking you further and further toward the destination you will design this week.

Let's get started on the homestretch to your Beautiful Money.

STEP ONE:
GOAL-SETTING GODDESS

In my twenties, I was often sent to conferences on behalf of the company I worked for, one of which taught the SMART goal program.

The SMART goal system is based on the idea that the easiest goals to achieve should be specific, measurable, attainable, realistic, and time based. At the company I worked for, everyone set SMART goals at the beginning of the year or quarter, and performance on these goals determined bonuses, promotions, and raises. I loved this program because it taught me, at a relatively young age, how to effectively set and achieve measurable goals in a systematic way.

When I quit my job, I realized that I could adapt the SMART goal system to help me reorganize my life and work toward more personal goals. After a few years, I nicknamed my method the DREAM goal system: dreamy, recorded, emotional, all-in, and measurable (we'll set DREAM goals soon). Like SMART goals, DREAM goals allow us to achieve by harnessing our focus, attention, and drive to get things done. But where SMART goals and DREAM goals differ is that DREAM goals use the power of our imagination to build the inspiration and momentum needed to put us in the state of action with the loving sense of urgency that's needed to achieve goals in a holistic way.

Most goal-setting techniques are logical. But when we are creating Beautiful Money, we want and need our heart to be involved. We need both our head and our heart in action to truly make DREAM goals a reality.

A CRASH COURSE IN DREAM GOALS

A DREAM goal is made up of five elements:

It's *dreamy*

A DREAM goal always inspires us and activates our imagination.

It's *recorded*

A DREAM goal is always recorded on paper (and audio too, if you feel inclined). Every DREAM goal should be recorded as a simple, clear, and powerful statement. Use phrases like "I have" and "I am" to further charge your DREAM goal with creative and activating energy. Your DREAM goal should also *always* have a deadline associated with it. We don't need to obsess about the exact date or get overly attached to it (more on that later), but a working deadline allows us to create a loving sense of urgency around the creative process.

It's *emotional*

A DREAM goal needs to be infused with excitement, energy, and a feeling in your gut that makes you a little hyper and excited to act.

It's *all-in*

A deep sense of commitment is needed to make any DREAM goal a reality. What I mean by "all-in" is that we are fully committed—mind, body, and soul—to do everything in our power with excellence in anticipation of achieving our DREAM.

It's *measurable*

The greatest lesson I took from my SMART goal training was to always ensure that goals are measurable. With time and experience, I realized that having dates associated with written goals often helps us to activate a sense of urgency. Because we have set a date, we tend to keep our eyes on the prize and our mind in the game. We prioritize better, work smarter, and are more mindful of how precious our time is.

Measurability helps us connect our dreams with space and time, but it is not everything. Remember, our imagination doesn't have a schedule. As Albert Einstein once said, "Logic will take you from A to B. Imagination will take you everywhere."[19]

Our DREAM goals are called that for a reason. We need to allow our imagination to run wild, to challenge our mind by living just outside our comfort zone, and to resolve to set and always move toward our DREAM goals to develop the resolve, focus, and discipline required for a truly fabulous, abundant, and fulfilling life.

When we set out to achieve great things—like when we set DREAM goals—we know that we are definitely going to face adversity. It's just how the universe works: it gives us on-schedule growth opportunities, at precisely the right time. Working through those challenges and staying focused on achieving our goals with purpose and intention helps us to develop resilience. It's a lot like being an elite athlete or an Olympian: we must actively train, persist, be disciplined, and develop the grit and character needed to receive the amazing abundance the universe has available for those who work hard and will use the wealth they build to benefit others. Moving toward your DREAM goal is kind of like doing your own mental marathon.

Our DREAM goals should push the envelope, challenge us to be on our toes, and require us to show up as our greatest selves on a daily basis. A true DREAM goal is one that makes your gut say yes! but that with overthinking might make your fear-based mind say no! Be mindful of listening to that initial gut response when you are creating your DREAM goal. Where DREAM goals are concerned, the gut always trumps the head!

THE BEAUTIFUL MONEY NUMBER: THREE

I find that creating and working on three DREAM goals at once is amazing because the spiritual and life force contained in the number three is powerful beyond language. I've always been drawn to the number three, but recently I revisited my astrological and numerological signs just for fun. I realized that one of my power numbers is three, but, even more important, according to AstroStyle.com, the number three is the "trinity number" combining "mind, body, and soul."[20] "Curiosity," "harmony," "transformation," and "fulfillment" are all words that have been associated with this fabulous number. For me, personally, seeing threes in my world does shift me into a truly abundant state. From a practical standpoint, I like working with the number three because it's pure and simple.

This is all to say that there is something truly magical about working in threes, which is why, when practicing Beautiful Money, we set three DREAM goals each year.

BECOME A DREAMER

Write out your three truly abundant, joyful, exhilarating, and inspiring DREAM goals for the next twelve months. These goals should absolutely challenge you and bring you outside your comfort zone but not paralyze you or prevent you from taking action due to fear or worry about how you're going to get them done.

Here are a few questions to help you get started:

What would be inspiring for you to complete or achieve?

What, when achieved, would make you feel on top of the world?

What, when achieved, would make you feel strong and confident?

What goal has your gut been telling you to commit to?

What goal are you not writing down because of fear?

What have you always dreamed about that felt just a little out of reach?

And here is a springboard for creating your first three DREAM goals:

Goal 1 should be an income goal for the year. Set a number that feels just out of reach. It should definitely be more than you're earning right now. Make this number a little scary but a lot exciting!

Your income goal is a perfect leadership measure because as your confidence, skills, and habits strengthen, your income will build. As we get to know ourselves better, and allow ourselves to get out of our own way, our income cannot help but bust at the seams. Oftentimes when we get comfortable and stop challenging ourselves to grow, our income gets complacent too and doesn't grow as much as we'd like— or at all!

Feel free to start with baby steps if it feels better. For example, if you earn $50,000 annually, expecting to earn $5 million within the next year is a stretch, but $75,000 or even $100,000 may not be, especially after you begin using what you've learned in this book. Remember to make goals that move you toward the fringe of fear but don't make you want to barf with fright.

Goal 2 should reflect one of your four pillars. For me, this is always a health-related goal. One year I set the goal of becoming a certified yoga teacher-trainer; another year I wanted to finish a full marathon. One of my clients, Scott, decided he wanted to set a new personal record at every major running-race distance, because fitness (especially running) is his passion. This second goal doesn't have to be health or activity driven per se, but it does need to reflect a core value.

Goal 3 should be a creative goal. It may be related to a dream you've had all your life, whether it's to quit a corporate job and become an entrepreneur, to buy property internationally, or simply to pursue a new career or passion. For me, publishing a book about Beautiful Money was a goal I worked on for many years.

Your third goal can be financially or business driven, especially if your dream is to live somewhere different or to open up a business. But this goal can also be creatively driven. Any creative gift you have—whether it's dance, writing, marketing, business, art, or music—has energy that can be channeled to make a dream a reality. My creativity often comes out in my business or my writing. My husband's creativity comes out in his music, art, and photography.

Keep in mind that the three goals you set in this final week of the Beautiful Money course should be things you've always wanted to do *and* things that make you feel like you are oozing with creative energy. This is not the time to play small or to chicken out about something you've always wanted to accomplish but are just a teeny-weeny bit afraid you'll never be able to achieve. This is the year you live big and brave and truly beautifully.

Beautiful Money Tip

*I*F YOU HAVE a big vision, that's awesome! But it's important to portion your huge, audacious dream into achievable steps. For instance, if your ultimate goal is to own a bed-and-breakfast, the goal for this year may be to select the city and neighborhood your B&B will be in or to have twenty thousand dollars saved by a specific date for the down payment.

Next year's goal could be to buy a property, and the following year to officially open for business. It's important to ensure your system for setting DREAM goals works for you. Some of us need more security, while others feel comfortable taking big risks. If smaller goals feel better in this moment, trust that! For me, goals need to be further out of my comfort zone than others might find appropriate. It's just how I roll. A friend of mine has a huge vision: she wants to become an online guru in her field of expertise, but her goal for the first year was to simply get her website up and running. Next year, she'll work on her social media platforms, marketing message, and building up an audience for her site.

It's always best to treat big, audacious goals as marathons, not sprints. Very few people wake up in the morning and decide, on the spur of the moment, to register for a 26.2-mile run. (I once registered just twelve hours before the start of the Toronto Marathon—and the results weren't pretty!) My point is that most of us have to build up both body and mind to achieve our big goals. Well before I ran my first marathon, in my early twenties, I set the simple goal of running a shorter race, an 8K. I still remember how I felt after completing it. Almost every inch of that race (and how I felt during it) is still fresh in my mind. It was a game changer for me. That one race rocked my world and inspired me to become a marathon runner. The following year, I set a goal of running both a half and full marathon. I was hooked!

It can help, too, to be specific about your three goals. "Save more" is a good start, but it's boring, it lacks life force, and it doesn't inspire. It isn't specific enough, nor is it dreamy! Instead, writing down, "By December 13, 2018, I will have successfully saved twenty thousand dollars to invest in my first income-generating property," will be much more specific, better aligned with your true mission, and more helpful in creating the motivation to make this dream a reality!

I keep my DREAM goals in a frame in my office so all three are right there in front of me. Take the year 2015 as an example. At the top of the page, I wrote, "I, Leanne Jacobs, am a deliberate creator in 2015 and focus my energy on the following three creations." Writing a sentence like that, in the present tense, and with amazing energy, is really powerful. It essentially states that you are ready and willing to challenge yourself, to break out of your comfort zone, to go after something you've always wanted but haven't fully committed to before. Once you are done with each goal, set the date you intend to achieve it by: maybe a year or nine months or six months from now.

It's also very important that each goal is simple to measure. You can have a yes/no measure or a quantitative measure (such as a financial target or other numeric value). Often my clients will have a few goals that are vague or too general (such as, "I am successful in my business"). When goals are vague or too general, it is difficult to determine if you were successful or not. What does "successful" mean? Be specific and clear about your goals so you can quickly and easily confirm their completion. And remember that you can always give yourself an extension, so don't get overly attached to the deadline. Sometimes divine timing has a different plan and doesn't work according to your schedule. Before you start to self-talk your way into a hole for not being good enough, just remember that in the game of life we often have to stop taking ourselves so seriously.

In 2015 I wrote:

Goal 1: By December 31, 2015, I joyfully achieve my abundant income goal for the year [I included a figure].

Goal 2: By July 1, 2015, I gratefully give birth to my happy, healthy baby.

Goal 3: By September 1, 2015, I successfully secure a global book deal for *Beautiful Money*.

I love to encourage clients to include their income goal as one of their annual DREAM goals because our annual income is a great leadership metric. It is also a great measure of how successfully you step out of your comfort zone and embrace change and transformation. Here are my client Faith's three audacious DREAM goals for 2016:

Goal 1: By December 31, 2016, I have successfully earned $100,000 (before taxes) at my own business.

Goal 2: By November 1, 2016, I have accumulated $25,000 in my real estate wealth account, which will be used as a down payment on a property.

Goal 3: By June 1, 2016, I have qualified for the Boston Marathon (3:40 marathon time).

Faith was already a successful entrepreneur, but she was ready to go for it and hit six figures for the first time. "It just feels magical to me, Leanne," she said. "It's not that much more than I'm earning now, but I just feel like hitting that benchmark will be a big breakthrough for me mentally and emotionally." The same could be said for Faith's goals of saving for a property, since she wanted to create equity and passive income through acquiring real estate. Finally, as a runner, Faith knew that qualifying for Boston was the pinnacle of the sport, and although it seemed a little out of reach for her present athletic ability, she figured it was worth striving for. "I've never not accomplished something I set out to do," she said, "so why not aim higher?"

Why not, indeed! Faith's goals are the perfect example of becoming a goal-setting goddess. Before practicing Beautiful Money, she probably never prioritized saving for a down payment or set an income goal for the year in January. The majority of people wait until the end of the year (or tax time) to review how much they made, instead of being proactive leadership and income-earning goddesses. When we practice Beautiful Money, we start with the end in mind—by committedly setting a powerful income goal before the year even starts!

Beautiful Money Tip

I HAVE A FEW additional tricks to share when it comes to creating and achieving your DREAM goals.

- ◆ Lead with imagination and creativity.
- ◆ If your intuition is telling you to pick a goal, don't let your head talk you out of it. That's just fear pretending to be your inner voice.
- ◆ *Always, always, always* write a DREAM goal down on paper. It's the easiest thing you can do to create momentum.
- ◆ Emotion is the true power for making dreams a reality. If you're not deeply inspired to make your written goal a reality, then that's not a DREAM goal.
- ◆ Keep your DREAM goal simple yet profoundly powerful.
- ◆ A true DREAM goal may bring up a little fear, but mostly your gut is churning with exhilaration (you may feel butterflies or get goose bumps). A common experience among my students is not being able to fall asleep after writing their DREAM goals down on paper. It's just too exciting to imagine that dream becoming a reality!
- ◆ Always set a deadline for completion but *never* get obsessively attached to that deadline. You're

not in control of divine timing. Your DREAM goal
may be meant to happen but not on the exact date
you've set.

◆ Pick a deadline, but be prepared to give yourself
extensions.

◆ Be loving and gentle with yourself (even though
you are a goal-setting goddess). Your DREAM
goals will happen at the right time. You're exactly
where you need to be.

◆ Share your DREAM goals with someone you love
and trust. Getting someone else's love and life
force behind your DREAM goal will only propel
you into greater momentum. (That said, select
someone who believes in you more than you believe in yourself and who oozes positivity, kindness, and authenticity.)

◆ Each DREAM goal should be loaded with life force,
love, and a deep desire to make the dream a reality. DREAM goals are alive and in the process of
being created the moment they get recorded on
paper.

◆ Expect a few detours, bumps, and bruises. To
achieve greatness, you must build up your resilience muscle. Along your journey, you will be fed
tests and challenges (and perhaps a few doses of
unkindness). You might even want to throw in the
towel on a few occasions. That's when you know
you're on the verge of something wonderful and
big. In my experience, the days that seem toughest
(when you bawl your eyes out and want to give up)
are the days right before a great transformation or
a leap forward toward making your goal a reality.
Hang in there, goal-setting goddess!

Now that we clearly understand how goals form a magical piece of the Beautiful Money journey, we can move on to our final, juicy exercise—mapping out how to make our dreams a reality.

THE BEAUTIFUL MONEY MAP

I have saved the Beautiful Money Map for our final exercise because it is where we put everything together. This is a visual road map that helps us along our path to holistic wealth and abundance. It visually calibrates our subconscious and conscious mind to stay on course and expands our imagination to help us see beyond the present and into our future. This is a visual tool that combines our path to wealth with our own unique habits for well-being and happiness.

My own Beautiful Money Map is my favorite piece of art in the house. It sits in a pretty frame on our bedroom dresser so I can gaze at it day and night. I absolutely adore my vision board, but my Beautiful Money Map shows me how I'm going to move toward making my vision board come to life. It is what pulls me toward my dreams, because it puts my vision board into words. If creating Beautiful Money and making our DREAM goals come true is a marathon, the Beautiful Money Map is the training plan we use to successfully traverse the course and cross the finish line.

The Beautiful Money Map uses your four pillars, your why, and the freedom dates you set during Weeks Two and Three to outline a plan of action for flowing toward Beautiful Money.

Keep in mind that our plan of action never ends up reflecting exactly how things happen. As we grow and create, we'll begin to see just how different the journey is from what we had expected. For the purposes of Beautiful Money, our plan is the message to the universe that we're ready to work, but the details are up to the universe. That's why it's crucial to create a plan (via the Beautiful

Money Map) but to remain open and flexible to how it may change over time.

When we create our own map, we not only carve out how we intend to take creative action but also prioritize our time with respect and appreciation. As you practice Beautiful Money, you will become more mindful of when it is time to take action and when it is time to rest. You will become more in tune with your body and your emotions, and realize that sometimes doing less helps you earn more. If you're totally exhausted and frustrated, taking a break or a vacation is likely the best Beautiful Money step you can take. If you're out of alignment, the Beautiful Money out there will likely find someone else to gravitate to.

The Beautiful Money Map is the culmination of all you've learned and defined for yourself so far. What we aim to do in creating this map is to practice being clear on our core values and our why so we can craft goals that align with those ideas and activities. This exercise maps out where we're headed, in terms of both personal growth and wealth. The Beautiful Money Map is a holistic snapshot of our core values, our financial goals, our passions, and the vehicles we'll use to dovetail the ideas that matter with the numbers we are aiming for.

For me to emotionally connect with anything, I need for the messages to be pretty visually. Our Beautiful Money Map (page 223) is created on a piece of bristol board and framed. It's the first thing Ric and I see when we wake up in the morning. It maps where we are going and what we're trying to create.

I created my Beautiful Money Map with my husband because family is one of my core values. In the past, I've sometimes been too independent, so I decided it would be a creative challenge for me to work with Ric. If you're in a relationship, you can choose to do your own map independently, as a couple, or even as a family if you've got older kids. If you're single, creating your map is like your first day of dream school!

While I'll provide some direction on how to create your Beautiful Money Map, there's no single way to do it. Feel free to be creative and to flow, and don't get hung up on specifics or how the Beautiful Money Map I did with my husband might be different from yours. Just remember that words contain powerful energy, so the words on your money map are going to be those that inspire and resonate with you for years to come; they should be light and positive.

Words that resonate for me include grace, abundance, happiness, peaceful, calm, mindful, quiet, silence, joy, prosperity, harmonious, love, yoga, health, meditation, organic, holistic, collective, team, tribe, family, healthy, health, movement, creation, nature, ocean, water, trees, animals, beauty, style, sail, travel, beach, forest, children, pray, and peace.

My husband and I chose to do a five-year map, but really you can choose whatever timeline and scope makes you feel challenged yet is short enough to let you see results. Keep in mind that your Beautiful Money Map is different from your three audacious goals and isn't usually something you redo every single year. DREAM goals are set each year, but a Beautiful Money Map has a wider scope. Ric and I redo ours every five years.

Again, feel free to find a scope that fits for you. Shorter timelines work well with my personality and keep me on my toes. If short timelines stress you out, give yourself the time and space you think you'll need to create your best life. Ideally, your map spans more than a year, to give you enough room to create and grow holistic wealth. But if your gut tells you a one-year Beautiful Money Map is right for you, go with that! Some of my clients like to do a ten-year map, but for me that creates too much distance.

I believe the universe likes speed but rewards patience. However, whatever timeline feels right to you is ultimately going to be the best for you and the universe.

There's no one right way to draw your map, so feel free to follow what I've done with my husband or to design your own. Ultimately, all you need to draw your own road map to abundance is pen and paper, the beginnings of a plan, and your imagination!

CREATE YOUR BEAUTIFUL MONEY MAP

*Take out a piece of paper and a pencil or pen

The paper can be anything—printer paper, notebook paper, canvas, poster board, bristol board (like mine), or stationery. Anything that makes you feel open to creativity is good. The same applies to the writing utensil—if there's a purple pen that you adore, or a calligraphy pen, use it!

*Create a column in the middle of the paper

Write your current net worth at the bottom of this column, and stack your goals for future years one by one above it.

So a five-year map that starts in 2016 would look like this:

Net worth:
2021: Goal
2020: Goal
2019: Goal
2018: Goal
2017: Goal

It's fun to dream about how far you might go, right? This middle column is your leadership report card. It's an objective, financially based evaluation of how far you've progressed on your Beautiful Money path. But remember, it's important not to attach too much value to hitting these exact targets. It's very unlikely that the future will happen just as you've sketched it out on this map. We want to avoid stressing out about "missing" these goals. Instead, we should think big, like visionaries do, and keep our eye on the broad picture. Start with the end in mind and then break the journey down into smaller mile markers.

In the beginning, I didn't even focus on how much money was coming in. I kept my mind on the larger target of being financially free. I kept my eyes on the prize. Today I treat my net worth as my leadership report card. Am I attached to the numbers? Not at all! Do I truly believe that everything will happen exactly as my map predicts? Probably not! But what I do know is that you have to start somewhere, and being clear is extremely important. If I continue to do the work and grow every day, I'll move toward the outcome the map outlines. If I don't hit my net worth goal for a given year, I just give myself an extension, because I expect to achieve that goal.

It might not happen exactly according to my timetable, but I will see my net worth reach or even surpass the numbers on my map. I just know that the numbers are on their way to becoming my reality (even if I don't see them yet) because, as we discussed during Week Two, expectation is *everything* when it comes to creating Beautiful Money.

In the space on one side of your net worth column write or draw your desires, passions, and favorite daily activities (sleep, yoga, running, reading, surfing, writing—anything)

These should be words that inspire you: your goals, your motivations, books you want to read, events, training, courses you plan to attend—whatever is fabulous and generates a huge smile on your face.

On the other side of the column write down your current financial vehicles and whatever income streams pique your interest that you might want to incorporate as part of your Beautiful Money plan; write down ways you can generate income, as well as current skills that can be used to create leverage

This is the strategic side of the map that clearly outlines your current and your intended additional streams of income (along with skills and activities that will generate Beautiful Money).

If you're working as a couple, you'll have to be creative in fitting everything together, for both of you, on each side of the net worth column. Dream big!

On the money map I did with Ric, I included things like publishing a book on Beautiful Money (!!), continuing to speak internationally to women about leadership, and being a leading global brand ambassador for health and wellness. Ric, who is a musician and real estate lover, wrote down his goals, including recording an album (which he did in the spring of 2016!), but he also has a passion for travel, writing, photography, architecture, and spiritual growth, so he wrote down not just the financial vehicles he currently has but also what's really in the works for the future, including land and animal preservation.

On my side, I listed the vehicles that inspire me to live better and to lead more every day. I know I need challenges to keep me growing, because if I saw boring or easy goals on my map every day, I would be tempted to be lazy!

My husband and I included sleep, juicing, taking our supplements, yoga, fitness, travel, music, and reading as some of our favorite activities. Any activity that fuels you with life force must make the Beautiful Money Map. Without these activities, making Beautiful Money would be seriously difficult, if not impossible.

Why? These activities help us feel fulfilled and most ourselves, and they fuel our body, mind, and soul to make us leaders. Remember, when we neglect these areas of our life, we will fill our day with stuff that doesn't fuel our soul and move out of alignment with Beautiful Money. We may chase money or "get" money, but we won't make joyful, aligned, and happy money. Adding activities to our map that make us feel whole and joyful helps us create clarity and live with purpose on a daily basis, because every time we see the map, we remind ourselves of what's truly important.

*At the very top of the map include your why (or words associated with it that are the basis for everything you do on a daily basis)

On our map, my husband and I included "healing and love on the planet" and "elevating consciousness" because that's why we get up in the morning. It doesn't mean that every day we're going to do a terrific job of those two things, but it does allow us to recenter and refocus if we have a few off-track days. It also serves as a reminder (when we are off track) to rest, refocus, and back to Beautiful Money "business."

The principles or ideas you include at the top of your map along with your why can be pretty simple. For instance, one of my clients wrote, "experiences are more important than things," because she wanted to remind herself how she's chosen to reprioritize what she spends money on. Feel free to also include a mantra, quote, or sentence that you absolutely adore.

IF YOU HAVE kids, include your vision for their family life as well!

Ric and I created an area at the bottom of our map where we outlined what we want to value as a family, like having an active, healthy lifestyle; providing an international and diverse classroom for our children; learning languages; to volunteer and do charity work as a family; and to always include leadership development as part of our children's education. We also want to teach our kids to always be generous and kind.

When our kids are old enough, we'll draw a map as a family so they can infuse their own creativity and imagination into our Beautiful Money Map. We can then be sure that we are all living with purpose and clear intentions. But even before that, a great practice to introduce the principles of Beautiful Money to your children can be to have kids of school age create their own vision boards every few months or annually. Perhaps they can also have space on your Beautiful Money Map to write words they associate with favorite activities, places, people, and things they love. This gets them in the habit of dreaming and doing early on in life.

As a general rule, it's up to you to decide what to include on your map in each category. I encourage you to be as creative and artistic as possible! I put my Beautiful Money Map in our bedroom so my husband and I can see it the moment we wake up. Looking at where we are headed lights up my soul, energizes me, and sets a clear intention and purpose for what I aim to do that day or that week or that month—and throughout my life in general. We positioned our map where the sun strikes early in the morning to literally help beam our map into reality.

The purpose of the Beautiful Money Map is to further clarify our goals and remind us of what we have set out to do with the precious time we have. When life gets hectic, it is easy to give up doing activities we love or that move us toward our greatest desires. We can, if we're not careful, easily get caught up in a trivial or uninspired life.

Even worse, we can end up living a life according to what other people want for us—a life we don't even feel is our own because we're so busy pleasing others and doing everything we can to fit in. Having this map where you can see it—whether that's in your bedroom, your office, or even your bathroom—will serve as a reminder of the life you have imagined and committed to.

When we look at our map, we should feel inspired by the words and goals on it. We know looking at our map that if we're moving toward our goals and acting with purpose, the numbers in the center column will happen.

We might not hit the timing perfectly, but as we grow, we will move closer and closer to our desired reality. The true power of our Beautiful Money Map is to help push us toward our goals by providing internal motivation every time we need it. One of the secrets to Beautiful Money is to learn to be self-motivated on a daily basis. Your map will help keep that motivation alive. You will wake up in the morning inspired and challenged and ready to take charge as the CEO of your life.

STEP TWO:
BECOME A MONEY MAGNET

Throughout this book, you've learned that to attract the best we need to align ourselves with, as well as contribute our best to, the world around us. Wealth is constantly flowing throughout the universe, and we have the power to decide, in our own internal landscape, whether to step into the flow. Remember, the universe is always watching us, to see how we act and react spiritually, emotionally, and financially to whatever is going on in our lives at any given moment. Nothing is really done in secret.

So how can we make sure that we are in Beautiful Money flow? A big aha moment for me was when one of my mentors said that once the money starts flowing, we will wonder where it has been in the past because the dollars will just pour in even though externally nothing much has changed. We're not doing anything different at work, but our results are exponentially more positive—because we've made an internal shift in our confidence to expect wealth and abundance. If someone were to come up to you and say you need $100,000 next month, you would be confident that you could make that happen. There's no question. To me, committing to being a Beautiful Money magnet is like a sacred vow we make to ourselves. This commitment is not just about the money. It's about being our most confident, kind, abundant, graceful, powerful, on-purpose, healthy, clear, aligned, joyful, and radiant self. Will we feel like this every day? No, but we believe it's possible and we commit to the journey. We treat ourselves respectfully and lovingly on the days we get off track, and we act as our own most devoted superfan to encourage ourselves back on course.

Becoming a money magnet serves both as a final lesson in practicing Beautiful Money and as a reminder to help us refocus and realign our energy when we inevitably become distracted by the chaos that life, our ego, other people, and the universe throw at us from time to time.

When you face an obstacle that you are not sure how to tackle—perhaps experiencing a huge change in your lifestyle like getting married or divorced, switching jobs, or (this happened to me!) having kids; or simply needing to refresh your momentum toward abundance—these money-magnet tips will help you get back on track to creating Beautiful Money.

1. Position Yourself for Wealth

Having clear financial and lifestyle goals provides a path to wealth, allows you to change and increase cash flow, and helps you create the internal momentum needed to practice the habits that create abundance long term. Surrounding yourself with the right people is also a key practice that will serve you well. You have to position yourself with the right people and the right goals.

Since the Beautiful Money program is designed to create clarity and momentum, revisiting the lessons in the book always positions you for wealth.

2. Study Wealth and Find Mentors

It's important to learn as much as you can. I love reading books on wealth, health, leadership, and spirituality. To me, they go hand in hand. What is important is that I am learning and growing every single day. I have found from experience that when I stop learning and growing (when I get caught up in my comfort zone or trivial things), the flow of Beautiful Money slows down.

I often ask the authors of financial books and blogs that I like to become my mentors. It may seem intimidating to reach out to an expert you admire, but often those leaders love to share pointers. Ask for their favorite tips or offer to buy dinner, a drink, or a coffee in exchange for their time. Maybe you can interview them (even for five minutes). You'll be surprised by the results. I have found that more people say yes than no.

If you need help in this area, reread the section on finding mentors ("More Thoughtful Tools") in Week Two and "Build a Beautiful Money Team" in Week Three.

3. You Are Paid in Direct Proportion to the Value You Create

This can be hard to hear, but usually we earn as much as we give. While it's impossible to be at the top of our game all the time, when we begin to see a drop in our overall income, it usually is a signal that we're also contributing less. Make sure that you're giving more than you are receiving. The universe will reward your generosity.

If you need help in this area, check out "The Beautiful Money Principles" in Week One.

4. Lead with Greatness in All You Do

Are you the CEO of your life? My mentors always seem to be challenging themselves without becoming frazzled. These people make generating income and creating a successful business simple. The secret to their success is clarity, focus, efficiency, and organization. Effective leaders don't let messes accumulate and certainly don't let clutter hold them back in life. Remember, truly successful people aren't busy just being busy. Truly successful people get shit done by prioritizing what's important, removing clutter, and avoiding chaos in their environments, social circles, and families, and throughout their lives in general.

The person in charge of you, at the end of the day, is you. Be the best CEO you can be in your home, at work, and with your family. Strive to reduce chaos, clutter, and time-wasting activities until your schedule feels open, light, and drama-free. Work efficiently and be a great boss to yourself, so you can make progress on becoming better and better every day. Make a list of the things that are holding you back in your life and work to remove them from your plate (hint: a few may be people).

If you need help in this area, focus on "The 80/20 Rule" in Week Three and "The Beautiful Money Cleanse" in Week One.

5. Focus on Results, Not Excuses

It is so easy to blame the external world and other people for what goes wrong. However, we know from practicing Beautiful Money that all results are created on the inside—namely, our internal environment.

We don't need to be hard on ourselves, but we should take full responsibility for what goes wrong and what goes right, both in business and in our personal lives. When things aren't going well or our lives aren't moving in the right direction toward wealth and abundance, we should take a minute to stop, eliminate excuses and blame (even of ourselves), and think about what we can do to produce the results we want, instead of what we don't. Barfing our stuff on other people will only prolong feelings of frustration and turn down (or off) the Beautiful Money taps.

We may all be prone to excusitis—yes, even me—but we should practice being mindful of this trap. When we stop blaming others or the world, we can practice refocusing our efforts on results, and achieve those results, instead of playing the blame game.

If you need help in this area, check out the section on page 240 on how to avoid becoming a money monster.

6. Have the Right Vehicles for Creating Wealth

One of the biggest challenges I see during my Beautiful Money workshops is people working really, really hard to grow financial vehicles that simply do not have the power to generate the type of income they desire (unless of course they are willing to burn the midnight oil and sacrifice their time and health—and even then it's often unlikely). Some students come to me because they want Beautiful Money but have absolutely no clue how to generate it. Some may have great incomes but are burning out chasing it. If these students can't work or don't want to work, their money stops. Some students make great money but they dislike (or even hate) what they do. Many come to me because they simply cannot grasp the concept of leverage. It's not Beautiful Money if you don't feel great (and healthy) making it!

We need to evaluate how we are creating holistic wealth and then strategically select income vehicles that work and that align with us. Tune in to what you want to achieve, and as a general rule, always choose the paths that set you up for success building, creating, and growing sustainable Beautiful Money.

If you need help in this area, check out the section on income streams under "Creating Holistic Wealth" in Week Three.

7. Be Crystal Clear About the Activities That Bring You Wealth

Managing money isn't all that difficult. We all know how to do it, but chaos and clutter want to steal our time, beauty, and money. To get to our next level, we need to refocus our time and energy on what actually makes us money and ignore the rest on a regular basis. This is a daily practice that will serve you well.

If you need help in this area, revisit the section on prioritizing profits in Week Three.

8. Create Space for Wealth and Avoid Chaos

Look at your schedule and pick out the distractions and time wasters. The ten hours you spend on Facebook or watching TV could be put to more productive and profitable use. Remove activities and time wasters to the best of your ability right now. Make space first, and then practice cleansing your life of time sucks whenever chaos creeps in (which will be often!).

If you need help in this area, revisit "The Beautiful Monday Time Tracker" in Week Three.

9. Create Systems, Leverage, and Networks

If you're evaluating a new vehicle or income stream, consider what you learned about how to create wealth. What are the systems that create income within this opportunity? Does the money invested create a consistent source of income? Do you make money as you sleep? Let a system do the work for you so you don't have to reinvent the wheel every time you have a new client or project. This can be as simple as creating scripts for e-mails you send frequently with the same content.

If you want a day or a week off just because you do, do you still get paid? What if you want to take a year off? Would you still generate income? At the end of the day, wealth is generated by either people at work or money at work. Make a commitment to learn more about ways you can earn income that don't require you to burn the midnight oil or do everything yourself. That's what leverage is.

Creating a network (or a tribe) today is fun and available to everyone. Creating an online presence and sharing your gifts with the world is accessible and available to anyone who has the desire. Tribes are powerful ways to create or join like-minded communities that are on course with your values and goals. The people within a tribe or network can also be very supportive and helpful as you grow your income, and they may even want to help support you and your gifts! We've all heard that it's not what you know, it's who you know—and that's representative of the truth that a network is powerful beyond measure.

If you need help in this area, read on. We'll discuss how to build leverage in detail very shortly.

10. **Design a Life (Because Life Is Too Short to Make a Living)**

Work to live. Don't live to work. If you have a dream or a goal you want to make a reality, learn what you need to know to achieve that goal. Remember, time is the only thing in life that we can never get back. Designing a lifestyle that makes us feel fulfilled, happy, and abundant is easy, but we have to commit to practicing what we've learned and to leading by example.

If you need help with this, reread "Goal-Setting Goddess" in step one.

11. **Always Start with the End in Mind**

When times get tough, you hit a rough patch, or you simply reach a plateau on the road to wealth, it's easy to become discouraged. Learn to focus your mind-set on your destination more than on what is happening in your day. This takes practice, but you will become really great at it. You are responsible for choosing which thoughts you accept as true. Learn to get good at tossing away ones that don't align with you and your destination.

There will always be days when we don't feel vibrant or aligned with our goals. But we need to practice mindfulness so we don't get distracted by our bad days, when all our anxieties kick up and we are tempted to live from a place of fear rather than from one of expectation. Our aim is to be focused on the end goal but to appreciate and live in the moment.

If you're struggling with this, check out "The Power of Now" in Week One and "Conquer Fear with Courage" in Week Two.

12. Embrace Mistakes and Divorce Perfection

Who cares if you fail? When we are in a fear-based mind-set we try to control everything around us—the environment, other people, our work situation—which not only causes us to hemorrhage energy but also blocks the creativity and flow that create greatness. Take risks, embrace your mistakes, learn from what you did wrong, and move on.

For help getting out of a fear-based mind-set, check out "Conquer Fear with Courage" in Week Two.

13. Cash Flow Is Queen

Always have a cash flow reserve—always! If we are starved for cash, it's hard to feel abundant and to soften into our feminine flow. And it absolutely messes with our money mind-set in a big way. It can cause us to get overly attached to our current state of lack and can make it difficult to expect that abundance is on its way. A chronic cash flow crisis hardens us on the inside and on the outside.

To learn how to increase cash flow, reread "Become Your Own Bank" in Week Three.

14. Save More, Spend Less—Now!

This is the core of Beautiful Money. The best time to start acting on the strategies in this book was yesterday—but we can act on our intentions today to be more mindful and have a better, more powerful, and healthier relationship with money tomorrow.

For help revising your finances and budget, check out "Become Your Own Bank" in Week Three.

15. Health Is a Money Magnet

The more you exude your unique radiant life force, the more people will be attracted to you without knowing specifically why. You're just cool, awesome, and inspiring, and people want to be in your presence! Putting your well-being first will help you rise to this state of magnetism. When we feel amazing on the inside, we shine brightly on the outside, and things will just seem to flow. If you want to make a better life for yourself, take better care of yourself. It will pay dividends not just financially, but spiritually, emotionally, and physically too.

DON'T BECOME A MONEY MONSTER!

All the tips I just shared will help you to live authentically and attract wealth and abundance like a magnet. Ideally, when we practice Beautiful Money, we create and grow wealth in a graceful and harmonious way, in which we don't negotiate our values or sacrifice kindness in order to have more zeros in our bank accounts. We bring others up with us as we rise. The Beautiful Money program is a collaborative one, not a competitive one.

But we all know a money monster. Money monsters come in all shapes and sizes but a common one we all know is the person who expects admiration and respect simply because he or she has accumulated a nice house, business success, a flashy car, a lot of stuff, and financial wealth. This is exactly the opposite of a Beautiful Money magnet.

Money can lead to a sense of superiority, entitlement, and competition. Building wealth can become an addiction. Once in a while, even a Beautiful Money student can be at risk of showing one or two money-monster traits. She may start out making money in a holistic way, but the moment the number of zeros in her bank account changes, her ego is at risk of taking over. Don't allow your ego to trick you into thinking that entitlement and superiority will serve you well.

ARE YOU BECOMING A MONEY MONSTER?

*T*HE BEAUTIFUL MONEY path is one on which we learn and grow as we go. No one is perfect, so the following list is a reminder of what we want to avoid doing while on our journey to holistic wealth. We are all works in progress and can fall victim to money-monster traits from time to time. These questions will help you reset your mind-set if you begin to creep into money-monster mode.

Are you losing your temper with people?

Are you beginning to be unkind to others?

Are you starting to feel like you don't have enough?

Are you giving up well-being or family time in pursuit of money?

Are you burning yourself out to earn money?

Are you feeling competitive and envious?

Are you hoarding money?

Are you choosing to be less generous?

Are you being deceitful?

Are you putting others down (with your words and actions)?

Are you feeling angry, depressed, frustrated, or unhappy?

Are you overspending?

Are you secretly feeling that you are better than others?

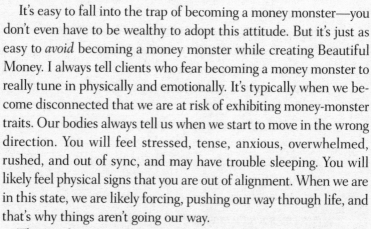

Are you treating people differently based on their wealth?

Are you feeling out of alignment with your true self?

Are you neglecting your family, health, or partner in pursuit of money?

Are you losing touch with your core values and yourself?

Do you have more fear about not having enough money or losing money?

Do you overpromise a lot?

Do you spend more than you save?

Are you constantly rushing and feeling behind?

Are you more focused on getting more than on giving more?

Are you thinking about your appearance and how others see you?

It's easy to fall into the trap of becoming a money monster—you don't even have to be wealthy to adopt this attitude. But it's just as easy to *avoid* becoming a money monster while creating Beautiful Money. I always tell clients who fear becoming a money monster to really tune in physically and emotionally. It's typically when we become disconnected that we are at risk of exhibiting money-monster traits. Our bodies always tell us when we start to move in the wrong direction. You will feel stressed, tense, anxious, overwhelmed, rushed, and out of sync, and may have trouble sleeping. You will likely feel physical signs that you are out of alignment. When we are in this state, we are likely forcing, pushing our way through life, and that's why things aren't going our way.

The good news is that you can always regroup and reroute to move in a more favorable direction. Every day is a new day and a fresh beginning. It's very easy for ambitious people like us to fall into this trap when we begin making money, to let our ego take over instead of leading from the heart. I know that when I pile too much on my plate, I lose connection with myself and with the world around me. I move out of a place of gratitude and into one of forcing my way forward. When we feel tense, jumpy, anxious, frustrated, angry, unkind, and pushy, and begin to project our shit onto other people or neglect to make time for our core values or activities that matter most, that's the money-monster mind-set approaching. Beautiful Money magnets are always happier, healthier, and more holistically abundant than money monsters! Money monsters may make a lot of money but at a huge cost.

Similarly, if you hoard money, become less generous (both financially and emotionally), feel defensive about your wealth or success, or start to feel envious of or competitive with peers, these are signals that you may be moving toward a money-monster mind-set out of the fear that there simply won't be enough money to go around. But we know as Beautiful Money practitioners that there's enough abundance for everyone.

HOW TO AVOID BECOMING A MONEY MONSTER

Here are some ways to kick our inner money monster to the curb:

◆ Give more than is expected
◆ Prioritize your core values
◆ Act with love and kindness
◆ View and treat others as you would like to be treated
◆ Respect every dollar you earn

- ◆ Seek out ways to serve more and give more
- ◆ Love yourself first
- ◆ Trust that there is more than enough abundance for everyone
- ◆ Trust that the universe has your back
- ◆ Do your best to stay present and connected
- ◆ Take care of yourself and sleep well at night
- ◆ Manage your money with excellence
- ◆ Celebrate success, even when others outshine you
- ◆ Remind yourself daily of all the gifts you have
- ◆ Practice gratitude

THE DOWNSIDE OF SUCCESS

Although this isn't the focus of Beautiful Money at all, I feel it is important to touch on the subject of "haters": people who love to knock others down in order to build their own confidence. In 2016, Fox News anchor Megyn Kelly wrote a great article for Motto.com (which I also contribute to) that pointed out how, in her opinion, most haters and people who criticize are bullies, motivated by envy.[21]

As Dr. Joseph Murphy points out in his amazing book *The Power of Your Subconscious Mind*, envy and jealousy are absolutely obstacles to the flow of abundance.[22] As you embark on your Beautiful Money journey, you will rise and make changes that others will witness and may see as threatening to their own confidence. Know that there is always the possibility that your friends and family members will say things that are unkind and meant to tear you down, not raise you up.

In my own life, I work to be mindful that these painful situations are actually opportunities to build up my own confidence, awareness, and resilience. It's crucial that we don't expend our energy and beautiful life force on people who don't deserve it. When you are faced with a hater, here's how to deal:

- Take a moment (or an hour or a day) to stroke your ego and acknowledge your heartbreak. I'm a very sensitive soul, so dealing with these situations is never one I look forward to.

- Recognize that your hater, whoever it is, has his own story and his own path. We don't always know what that person is dealing with in his life, no matter how close we think we are or how much we believe we know.

- Detach from the trivia of the situation and practice seeing the situation symbolically (as Caroline Myss teaches in her *Call to Live a Symbolic Life* workshop).[23] See your daily experiences as great life lessons that strengthen you. Be the kinder and bigger person. Offer up love and support, either to the universe or in person. You will face resistance, because showing kindness and empathy is not what your ego wants to do. Your ego wants to spew unkind language and tell the hater how you really feel. This is why dealing with haters is such a juicy teaching opportunity for confidence.

- With time and practice, you will get better at ignoring haters and not getting caught up in their web of drama. You will take some time to feel wounded and hurt, but your greater, more enlightened self will move on quickly and see the game in it all. Haters need our love and compassion, and only feed on our reaction. Don't play their game; rise above it. Living well is always the best revenge.

- When you feel ready, move the energy out of your body. Go for a workout, a yoga class, or a dance class. Get those stirred-up issues out of your tissues so you can regain beautiful space and calmness. You may also choose to tell a friend or two about the experience, but don't make this a habit. Circulating the situation among friends and community will only keep the drama alive. Aim to let it go, through either physical activity or a spiritual practice like meditation.

Ultimately, Beautiful Money is about positivity and living well, not getting caught up in the drama of chasing external success. When we shift our mind-set to becoming money magnets, we set ourselves up both to create wealth for ourselves and to make positive change throughout the world.

STEP THREE: AUTHENTICALLY HOLISTIC

I've been teaching the Beautiful Money course for years, but when I sat down to write this book, I realized that the program centers on four key concepts:

- Leadership
- Leverage
- Legacy
- Love

These four concepts lead Beautiful Money. Not only do the words vibrate with powerful and radiant energy but they contain the keys to creating long-term holistic wealth. If I had only a few minutes to teach Beautiful Money, I would focus on these four concepts. They summarize everything we've discussed so far and help you to easily identify where your time and energy should be focused. I believe that when we focus our attention and our thoughts on leadership, leverage, legacy, and love we simply can-

Beautiful Money
THE 4 L'S

LEADERSHIP	LEVERAGE
Results	Studying wealth
Boundaries	Passive income streams
Goal-setting mastery	How to leverage yourself
Time management	Doing more with less
Visionary process	Setting yourself up to thrive
action + allowing process	Avoiding adrenal fatigue
	Why your health needs leverage

LEGACY	LOVE
Tax strategies	Creativity
Insurance plans	Purpose
Investments	Core values
Cash flow	Meaning
Beautfiul Money Map	Fulfillment
Money management	Contribution
Wealth planning	Intuition
Kids, families, and money	Self-esteem
	Faith

not fail. When we bake with these ingredients, a superdecadent Beautiful Money masterpiece must come out of the oven.

This is the best way to practice Beautiful Money on an everyday basis and truly live a holistic, authentic life. The four L's encompass everything that you've learned in this book. Your work is now to identify which key area (or two) speaks to you most and is seeking your attention right now in your life. For many of my friends and clients who are parents, legacy speaks loudest at this point in their lives. Ever since I was a kid, I have been committed to leadership. You may have lots of love in your life, but I am asking you to expand on how greatly you shine this love into the world. On days when you feel crappy or down, these are the moments the universe is asking you to shine your love. It's easy to shine love when you feel amazing, but your practice is to shine it more on the days when you don't feel like it.

This is my current practice. I am always focused on all four concepts, but if I had to pick one, love would always be my first choice. The great news is that all four of the L's work together to create a Beautiful Money life! You don't have to choose just one out of the four. You might, however, have a personal short-term focus depending on how you feel or your current situation. If you are recently divorced, for example, leadership and love (self-love) might be given a little higher priority as you get back on your feet and deepen your connection and relationship with yourself.

Once you have selected a priority (or two) for right now, you can focus your energy and attention on that concept (or two) for the next month, six months, or year. It's amazing to see how quickly we can move toward a greater state of knowing and awareness.

Beautiful Money Tip

I AM ALWAYS EAGER to participate in personal development courses or to read the latest self-help book. By focusing on one or two key areas—like love and leadership—I'm actually able to home in on what I really want to learn about and, as a result, spend less time and money trying to learn everything about . . . well, everything! It's a great way to maximize a desire to learn with a commitment to creating Beautiful Money.

Leadership

The easiest way for me to describe leadership is letting your most powerful, authentic, and loving self out for the world to see. I believe leadership is everything. To me, leadership is not the words that come out of your mouth but the person you are. It's about what you do with your life and how you present yourself to the world, starting with how you lead your own life first. I have always admired parents who lead their children by example, who show them the way to live instead of just telling them.

Leadership is about how you show up in and connect with the world around you. It's about how committed you are to owning your own experiences rather than projecting your shit on other people. It's about how much you deeply understand that love overpowers ego and how that discovery can lead to peace and grace. Leadership is how you show up in the world on your worst days. It's easy to lead when all is going great.

If you are interested in leadership, consider these questions: How do you act on your worst days? How do you treat others when you're having a truly bad day? How committed to excellence are you when no one is watching and when you feel like crap? There are so many books I adore on leadership if you're just getting started, like *The 21 Irrefutable Laws of Leadership* by John Maxwell, *The 7 Habits of Highly Effective People* by Stephen Covey, and *Think and Grow Rich* by Napoleon Hill.

Leading by example is a simple way to incorporate this quadrant of the Beautiful Money circle into your life. When presented with a situation you don't know how to handle, whether practical or emotional, think: What would I tell my closest friend or my child to do? In most situations, we already know the answer. We already know how to lead. The hardest part is often taking action because that means we give up the easier role of being a follower. Leadership is about taking full responsibility for our lives, even when things aren't going our way. It is about mindfulness and generosity and kindness. Great leaders don't spend major time on minor things. Leaders fill space and time with loving thoughts and delicious actions.

Everyone is in a position to lead. Leading by example, taking the driver's seat in your life, and mindfully respecting your finances are all keys to Beautiful Money. There are opportunities every day for us to stop being followers, to create healthy boundaries, and to step into our greatest lives by being our best and most courageous selves. Most people fear committing fully to leadership because it means they can no longer blame anyone else. They have to be committed to owning every result in their lives, which isn't always easy and definitely not always fun! This is yet another example of why most people default to "fine," as we discussed earlier. When we're fine, we don't have to lead. But if we want to truly create Beautiful Money, we need to step into our own leadership and own it.

Leverage

This is the big ticket, baby. There are two kinds of leverage that most of us lack in both our personal and professional lives: time leverage and financial leverage. If you're a perfectionist or a control freak, or you fall victim to the "if I want it done right, I have to do it" school of thought, you probably seriously lack time leverage. You may feel constantly tense, rushed, or frustrated. You may project your shit onto others when you are having a bad day (or even a good day) because your cup isn't just full; it's spilling over.

Everyone needs space, peace, and calm in their life. When we don't have leverage—with our time or our money—we end up burning out. Financial leverage is likely missing from your life if you don't make money while you are sleeping. If your income didn't go up while you were on a weekend away, or while you were doing something else, it's time to tweak what you're doing with your money.

Leverage comes down to either people at work or money at work. Essentially, this quadrant of Beautiful Money is about working smarter instead of working longer or harder. Real estate, investing, direct selling, and affiliate and membership programs are some of the popular ways to infuse your life with leverage. The first three are the most popular. The vehicle for leverage you choose will likely depend on your lifestyle, how much you have to invest, and what interests you. My husband and I focus our attention on the first three. These align well with our values and our bohemian ways.

The Beautiful Money program will help you make space for what you truly want to do by creating leverage everywhere leverage is possible. At home, this might mean not trying to do everything yourself. It might mean you give your roommate, spouse, or children a chore list and do not worry so much whether everything gets done perfectly. (If you are freaking out right now about even the *idea* of this, I totally get it.) Or perhaps if you have the money, you could hire a housekeeper or a landscaper to take care of the work for you. In my case, I want to spend the majority of my time with my family. I don't want to spend hours cleaning and cutting the grass when I could be hanging out with my hunky husband or my awesome kids—so I gave in a little on my standards of how clean our house should be and hired a housekeeper.

What is most important to note is that when leverage is your hot concept for right now, you want to think of creating it in a holistic way. Consider every inch of your life and the ways you can generate greater leverage or room to breathe. How can you create way more by doing much less? This will be your new favorite question!

For most of my clients (especially women), the toughest part of embracing leverage is learning how to ask for help. This seems so simple but has been proven to be the most difficult assignment for almost all my clients (including myself). I'm not sure what we're all so scared of, but asking for help is the key to holistic wealth and well-being. Start small today by asking your partner or friend if he or she can do something for you. And notice what feelings show up when you do it. When I first did this, it was totally out of my comfort zone. I had never asked for help before! But when I considered where that had got me—broke and burned out—I figured that I had to let go in order to create the leverage I needed.

When everything in our lives is dependent on us being there or doing something, we have zero leverage and become disconnected from our heart and our truth. We become busy being busy and often lose the simplicity and peacefulness that creates joy. By practicing asking for help and delegating tasks that other people are capable of doing for us, we can create more space and time to do what we truly love. And we can create more wealth and happiness in the process. That's what leverage is really all about.

Legacy

What do you want to be known for? How will you leave the world a better place? Would you like your work to positively impact the world long after you're gone? What is the legacy you'd like to leave to your family? A lot of us don't want to think about the day when we will no longer be here, but it's crucial to start thinking about what we'll leave behind and what situation others will be in because of our attention (or lack of attention) to our financial landscape.

A legacy can be financial, but it doesn't have to be. For example, a lot of people associate the word with providing funds for children and grandchildren, but a legacy can be as simple as establishing an internship at your company, a scholarship at your alma mater, or a consistent volunteer group at a charity. My definition of a legacy is the contribution you make to other people and to the world at large. It is the beautiful energy you create that circulates even when you're not around. And because everything is energy, there are infinite ways for you to create your very own legacy that you leave to the world. If you desire to write a book or record a song, your work will circulate long after you are gone. It's such a powerful concept to think about.

When we start thinking about our legacy and what will happen in the future, it's easy to see whether the life we're living today dovetails with what we want to be remembered for—and whether we need to correct our course. Here is a simple list of ideas to help get you thinking about your beautiful legacy:

- Are you interested in volunteering or starting a charity?
- Would you like to invest in a new company that you believe in?
- Do you have smart investing strategies in place for your family (whole life plans, par plans, trusts, investments, education funds, wills, and a power of attorney)?
- Do you have a current income stream you can assign to a family member or children in your will? (This is a key reason direct-selling businesses are popular.)
- Have you spoken to a financial expert about tax implications for the legacy you're building? (This is especially important if you own your own company or have a big real estate portfolio.)
- Would you love to write a book, create a podcast, record an album, run a fund-raiser, or sponsor a child?
- Would you like to serve another country through a mission or not-for-profit project?
- What are some big dreams you have for contributing to the world?
- What do you want to share with others? (Journaling or recording your wisdom for family and for future generations is an amazing idea.)

My starting place when I focused on building my legacy was to make sure that no one would be negatively impacted financially if something unexpected happened to me. Setting up a meeting with a tax specialist, an insurance specialist, and a financial specialist is a great place to start if this is your goal. At the time, I had heard a horror story about a friend's father passing away without a will in place, which created a ton of stress and tension among his grieving family. I didn't want that for my family, so I created a will, designated power of attorney, and purchased a healthy amount of life insurance. Once that foundation was set, I began (and continue) to build on it, so if something does happen to me, my legacy is in place.

Love

Love is the very foundation of truth and of Beautiful Money. When we are disconnected from love, nothing works well. We might create businesses and make money but it will cost too much. If we lack joy, peace, health, and calmness, there's not a lot to be gained from being wealthy.

In the Western world, we rely so much on our minds that we tend to neglect our hearts. This is when things get messy. We're trained through the education system to be fabulous at following the crowd and taking direction. We are trained from a young age to value our intellect and logical reasoning over feelings and intuition. We live with internal tension created between the brain and the heart. Our hearts seek connection, freedom, and expansion while our minds want to keep us orderly, analytical, and predictable. To truly tap into our own power and live out our destiny, we must learn to trust our intuition and better listen to our heart.

My true purpose in writing this book is to guide you to shine as brightly as you desire and to vibrate with life force like never before. This takes time, practice, and patience. It also requires a deep commitment to loving yourself most. Self-love and developing the most delicious and healthy self-esteem must be your number one priority. When this isn't the first priority, your relationships, your business, and your life lack a healthy foundation. Whether you want to create a booming business, find your soul mate, create Beautiful Money, or just live your most authentic, connected life, loving yourself unconditionally is home base. As Pema Chödrön said, "Compassion for others begins with kindness to ourselves."[24]

When we love ourselves greatly, we have the power within ourselves to create whatever we want. We can choose action despite fear and become a courageous force of inspiration for others. When we love ourselves first, unconditionally, we will love and appreciate the world around us beyond measure. When we love ourselves first, we are destined to make Beautiful Money.

Choose love over fear.

Choose love over unkindness.

Choose love over frustration.

Choose love over stuff.

Choose love over everything—

And you will live a truly beautiful, fulfilling, great, abundant life.

NOTES

INTRODUCTION

1. www.cbsnews.com/news/why-25-million-middle-class-americans-live-hand-to-mouth/.

WEEK ONE: MAKE GORGEOUS SPACE

2. www.usatoday.com/story/money/personalfinance/2015/12/07/how-clean-up-your-credit-report/76006334/.
3. www.nerdwallet.com/blog/credit-score/credit-score-range-bad-to-excellent/.
4. www.thesimpledollar.com/how-to-calculate-your-net-worth/.

WEEK TWO: YOUR BEAUTIFUL MIND

5. Henry Ford with Samuel Crowther, *My Life and Work* (Garden City, NY: Doubleday, Page & Company, 1923).
6. www.youtube.com/watch?v=Lp7E973zozc.
7. www.psychologytoday.com/blog/focus-forgiveness/201307/conscious-the-unconscious.
8. Rollin McCraty, PhD, "The Energetic Heart: Bioelectromagnetic Communication Within and Between People," in *Clinical Applications of Bioelectromagnetic Medicine*, eds. P. J. Rosch and M. S. Markov (New York: Marcel Dekker, 2004), 541–62.
9. www.merriam-webster.com/dictionary/affirm.
10. T. Epton, P. R. Harris et al., "The Impact of Self-affirmation on Health-Behavior Change: A Meta-analysis," *Health Psychology* 34, no. 3 (2015), 187–96. Retrieved from www.ncbi.nlm.nih.gov/pubmed/25133846.
11. J. David Creswell et al., "Self-Affirmation Improves Problem-Solving under Stress," *PLoS One* 8, no. 5. Retrieved from http://journals.plos.org/plosone/article?id=10.1371/journal.pone.0062593#abstract0.
12. Dr. Joseph Murphy, *The Power of Your Subconscious Mind* (Floyd, VA: Wilder Publications, 2008).
13. Benjamin Mee, *We Bought a Zoo* (New York: Weinstein Books, 2008).

WEEK THREE: BECOME AN ACTION HEROINE

14. Wayne Dyer, *Living the Wisdom of the Tao* (Carlsbad, CA: Hay House, 2008), 77.
15. www.huffingtonpost.com/stephanie-seibel/dr-wayne-dyer-lives-on_b_8080952
    .html.
16. www.oprah.com/own-super-soul-sunday/Dr-Brene-Brown-on-Faking
    -It-Perfectionism-and-Fear-Video.
17. Liz Weston, *The 10 Commandments of Money* (New York: Hudson Street Press,
    2011), 155.
18. Available via www.jimrohn.com.

WEEK FOUR: DESIGN YOUR DESTINATION

19. Albert Einstein, *The World As I See It* (New York: Citadel, 2006).
20. http://astrostyle.com/master-numbers/.
21. http://motto.time.com/4203136/megyn-kelly-deal-with-haters/.
22. Murphy, *The Power of Your Subconscious Mind*.
23. Caroline Myss, *The Call to Live a Symbolic Life* (audio CD workshop) (Carlsbad,
    CA: Hay House, 2004).
24. Pema Chödrön, *Start Where You Are* (Boulder, CO: Shambhala Publications,
    2001).

INDEX

Note: Page numbers in italics refer to illustrations.

Leanne Jacobs is a holistic wealth expert and leadership mentor. She has worked in sales and marketing for several *Fortune* 500 and *Fortune* Global 500 companies, including Johnson & Johnson, Nike, DuPont, and L'Oréal. She holds a BS in biomedical toxicology, as well as an MBA. She is a certified clinical nutritionist and a certified Pilates and yoga instructor. Leanne and her husband are parents to four children and spend their time traveling, pursuing their passions, and contributing as cofounders to the World Healing Academy.

If you enjoyed this book, visit

www.tarcherperigee.com

and sign up for TarcherPerigee's e-newsletter to receive special offers, updates on hot new releases, and articles containing the information you need to live the life you want.

tarcherperigee

LEARN. CREATE. GROW.

Connect with the TarcherPerigee Community

· · ·

Stay in touch with favorite authors

Enter giveaway promotions

Read exclusive excerpts

Voice your opinions

Follow us

f TarcherPerigee

🐦 @TarcherPerigee

📷 @TarcherPerigee

If you would like to place a bulk order of this book, call 1-800-733-3000.